# THE AUTUMN GARDEN

# GARDEN

BY LILLIAN HELLMAN

★

★

DRAMATISTS
PLAY SERVICE
INC.

THE AUTUMN GARDEN was first produced by Kermit Bloomgarden at the Coronet Theatre, New York City, on March 7, 1951. It was directed by Harold Clurman and the setting and lighting were by Howard Bay. The cast was as follows:

| | |
|---|---|
| ROSE GRIGGS | Florence Eldridge |
| MRS. MARY ELLIS | Ethel Griffies |
| GENERAL BENJAMIN GRIGGS | Colin Keith-Johnston |
| EDWARD CROSSMAN | Kent Smith |
| FREDERICK ELLIS | James Lipton |
| CARRIE ELLIS | Margaret Barker |
| SOPHIE TUCKERMAN | Joan Lorring |
| LEON | Maxwell Glanville |
| CONSTANCE TUCKERMAN | Carol Goodner |
| NICHOLAS DENERY | Fredric March |
| NINA DENERY | Jane Wyatt |
| HILDA | Lois Holmes |

The time is September, 1949. The place is the Tuckerman house in a summer resort on the Gulf of Mexico, about 100 miles from New Orleans.

## ACT I
Thursday night after dinner.

## ACT II
SCENE 1. The following Sunday morning.
SCENE 2. That night.

## ACT III
Early the next morning.

# THE AUTUMN GARDEN

## ACT I

SCENE: *The Juckerman house in a town on the Gulf of Mexico, a hundred miles from New Orleans. A September evening, 1949, after dinner. The scene is the living-room of the house. To the R. and to the L. of living-room are side porches, separated from the room by glass doors. Upstage R. is a door leading into entrance hall of house: through this we can see hall and stair-case. On porches are chairs and tables. The furniture of the living-room is handsome but a little shabby. It is all inherited from another day.*

AT RISE: GENERAL GRIGGS, *a good-looking man of about fifty-three, is sitting on chair L. of sofa, reading a book.* ROSE GRIGGS, *his wife, is an ex-pretty, soft-looking woman of about forty-three,* CARRIE ELLIS, *sitting D. R., is a rather distinguished-looking woman of about forty-five. Both ladies have on dinner clothes:* ROSE'S *dress is too young for her, and too fancy,* CARRIE'S *dress is, like* CARRIE, *handsome and dignified.* MRS. MARY ELLIS *is sitting L. of table R. C. Across from it her grandson,* FREDERICK ELLIS. MRS. ELLIS *is a woman in her seventies, sprightly in manner and movement when she wishes to be: broken and senile when she wishes to seem broken and senile.* FREDERICK ELLIS *is a pleasant-looking young man of about twenty-five. He is reading proof-sheets of a MS, occasionally making a correction. On L. porch* EDWARD CROSSMAN *is sitting alone. He is a man of about forty-six or seven, tired and worn-looking, as if he were not in good health. There is silence for a second after the curtain goes up.* ROSE, *singing, crosses U. to hall, looks U. L., then crosses D. and sits sofa.* FRED *puts a galley-proof on table,* MRS. ELLIS *picks it up.* FRED *takes it from her, puts it down again.* ROSE *laughs, stops singing and speaks.*

ROSE. Now where is it? Everything's been so topsy-turvey all evening. If I can't have it immediately after dinner, then I just about don't want it. At home you can bet it's right waiting for us when we leave the dining-room, isn't it, Ben? (*He looks up, then back to paper. She sings few more notes.*) Too bad it's Thursday. I'd almost rather go and see *him* than go to the party. (MRS. ELLIS *looks at her. To* MRS. ELLIS, *being solicitous.*) I think it's what keeps you awake, Mrs. Ellis. I mean a little is good for your heart, the doctor told me always to have a little, but my goodness the amount you have every night.

MRS. ELLIS. (*Dryly. Pleasantly.*) Would you mind telling me what you're talking about, Mrs. Griggs? You said if it wasn't for the party you'd go and see *him,* but you thought *I* drank too much on a Thursday?

ROSE. (*Giggles.*) Coffee. I mean you drink too much coffee.

MRS. ELLIS. Then it is *coffee* you wish to go and see?

ROSE. (*Laughing.*) Now, now. You're teasing. (*Now serious.*) You know very well I mean Robert Taylor in that thing.

MRS. ELLIS. Believe me, I did *not* know you meant Robert Taylor in that thing. You know, General Griggs, after seven summers I have come to the conclusion that your wife considers it vulgar to mention anything by name. There's nothing particularly genteel about pronouns, my dear.

ROSE. (*Rises, crossing* L. *to* C. *At* C., *pleasantly.*) I know. It's a naughty habit. Ben has been telling me for years. (*Crosses* L. *to above sofa.*) Do you like my dress, Ben?

GRIGGS. (*Distracted.*) It's nice. (CROSSMAN *rises, crosses* U., *gets ash-tray from porch table.*)

ROSE. (*To* BEN.) Have I too much rouge? (*Crosses* R. *to* C. *To others.*) Know what *she* used to say? (*Quickly.*) Ben's mother, I mean. (*Crosses* L. *above sofa.*) She used to say it before she died. (*Sees* CROSSMAN. *To* CROSSMAN.) Come and join us. (*To others. Crosses* R. *above sofa.*) She used to say that Southern women painted a triangle of rouge on their faces as if they were going out to square the hypotenuse. (*Pause.* MRS. ELLIS *looks at her.*) Ben came from Philadelphia, and his mother was sometimes a little

6

sharp about Southerners. (*Crosses* L. *to doors.* CROSSMAN *crosses* D. *Sits in* L. *porch chair.*)

MRS. ELLIS. (*To* CARRIE; *smiling.*) Who could have blamed her?

ROSE. (*Back to* CROSSMAN; *in door.*) Know what she told me last winter when I met her at the Club?

CROSSMAN. (*Turns, smiles.*) Ben's mother?

ROSE. (*Admonishing and flirting.*) No. Your sister, of course. She said we see more of you here on your summer vacation than she sees all year round in New Orleans. She says you're getting to be a regular old hermit. You have to watch that as you get older. You might get to like being alone—and that's dangerous.

MRS. ELLIS. I used to like being alone. When you get old, of course, then you don't any more. (ROSE *crosses* D., *sits on* R. *end of sofa, facing* R.) But somewhere in the middle years, it's fine to be alone. (GRIGGS *stops reading. Pointedly, to* GRIGGS. *Very quickly.*) Happiest year of my life was when my husband died. (ROSE *reacts.*) Every month was spring-time and every day I seemed to be tipsy, as if my blood had turned a lovely *vin rosé*.

CARRIE. (*Rises, crossing* U. *to above* FREDERICK.) You're lyrical, Mother. (*Fixes rosette in* FREDERICK'S *lapel.*)

MRS. ELLIS. (*To* FREDERICK, *chuckling.*) Do you know I almost divorced your grandfather, Frederick? During the racing season in 1901. (*Phone rings.* ROSE *crosses below phone table, and answers it.*)

FREDERICK. (*Looks up, laughs.*) You don't feel it's a little late to talk about it?

MRS. ELLIS. Thought you might like to write my biography—when you're finished with regional poetry.

ROSE. (*Into phone.*) Hello. (SOPHIE *comes into room from hall to answer it.* ROSE *hands phone to* SOPHIE.)

SOPHIE. (*Into phone. They all listen.*) Yes? No, sir. We do not take transient guests, only permanent summer guests. No, never, sir. You might telephone to Mrs. Prescott in the village. Thank you, sir.

ROSE. Dear Sophie, where *is* coffee? (SOPHIE *comes to hall door. She is a plain-looking, shy girl of about seventeen. She has a hesitant, over-polite manner and speaks with a slight accent. She has on a party dress, almost all of which is covered by a kitchen apron.*)

SOPHIE. Aunt Constance is most sorry for the delay. We bring it immediately. (*She disappears* U.)

ROSE. (*Crossing* R. *to* R. *of sofa. With a lift in speech.*) Frederick, do you know I've been giving Sophie dancing lessons, or trying to? (FREDERICK *puts galley-proofs on table.* MRS. ELLIS *picks them up, reads.*) She's a charming child, your intended, but she's never going to be a dancer. (CARRIE *crosses* D. R.)

FREDERICK. (*Pleasantly.*) Did you tell Mrs. Griggs, Mother? I thought we agreed that since there were no definite plans as yet ——

CARRIE. (*Sits* D. R. *A little uncomfortable.*) It's natural that I should speak about my son's marriage, isn't it?

ROSE. (*At* L. *of chair* L. *of table.*) Why, goodness, yes indeed it is. I'd have felt hurt ——

GRIGGS. Don't you know that women have no honor, Frederick, when it comes to keeping secrets about marriage or cancer?

FREDERICK. (*Looks at* MRS. ELLIS, *but it is a self-reproach.*) No, sir. I didn't know. I'm too young for my age.

MRS. ELLIS. (*Who has been busy reading. Intervening. Puts proofs on table.*) I know that I'm too young to be reading Payson's book. Full of the most confused sex. (ROSE *crosses* R. *to above table, glances at galley-proofs* FREDERICK *is holding, then steps up stage a step.*) I can't tell who is what. And all out of doors. Is that new, so much sex out of doors? Is it, General?

GRIGGS. I don't think it's a question of "new." I think it's a question of climate.

MRS. ELLIS. (*Points to book.*) But aren't sexual relations the way they used to be: between *men and women?* It's so twitched about in Mr. Payson's book. You know, I think the whole country is changing.

GRIGGS. (*As if he wished to help* FREDERICK.) Has Payson written a good book, Fred?

FREDERICK. It's a *wonderful* book. I think he's going to be the most important young writer ——

CARRIE. You said the first two books were wonderful, Frederick. And they didn't sell very well.

MRS. ELLIS. I don't know why they didn't—I always thought houses of prostitution had a big lending-library trade. (ROSE *crosses* L., *sits phone chair.* FREDERICK *gets up, as if he were angry, takes galley-proofs, stops below his chair.*)

8

CARRIE. Will this new book sell, Frederick?

FREDERICK. (Slightly irritated.) I don't know, Mother. (Crosses R. to door.)

CARRIE. I hope it sells. Any man is better off supporting himself.

FREDERICK. (Crosses L. to L. of D. R. chair. Smiles.) Mother, sometimes I think no people are quite so moral about money as those who clip coupons for a living.

MRS. ELLIS. (Putting them in their places.) And why not? Particularly your mother, who is given the coupons already clipped by me who has the hardship of clipping them. That leaves her more time to grow moral. And then, of course, you who don't even have that much trouble are left at leisure to be moral about those who have to live on unearned money.

CARRIE. (Puts out cigarette. Rises, crosses U. to D. R. of table. Putting MRS. ELLIS in her place, to GENERAL GRIGGS.) You mustn't look uncomfortable, General. You should know by this time that my mother-in-law enjoys discussing family matters in public. (CARRIE sits R. of table. FREDERICK crosses U., sits chair U. R., reads proofs.)

GRIGGS. Do I look uncomfortable? I was thinking how hard it is to be young.

ROSE. (To GRIGGS.) Won't you come to the party? (To others.) Ben has never gone to the Carter party. I am sure they're just as insulted every year ——

GRIGGS. (Smiling.) I don't think so.

ROSE. (Being a good wife.) But what will you do with yourself? Why don't you go to see Robert Taylor? It's that war picture where he does so well and you'll want to see if it's accurate.

GRIGGS. (Smiling.) No. I don't want to see if it's accurate.

ROSE. (Rises, crosses D. to above sofa.) Do you like my dress?

GRIGGS. (With pleasant finality.) It's nice.

MRS. ELLIS. You are a patient man. (To ROSE.) Do you know you've asked him that five times since rising from dinner?

ROSE. (Crosses R. above to L. of MRS. ELLIS.) Well, I feel young and gay, and I'm going to a party. I wish the Denerys would come before we leave. I like meeting new people and they sound so interesting. I thought they were supposed to arrive in time for dinner. (Slight pause. To CARRIE.) Is he absolutely fascinating?

CARRIE. I don't know, Mrs. Griggs. I haven't seen him in twenty years or more.

9

ROSE. (*Crosses* L *to door. Calling to* CROSSMAN.) Is he fascinating, Mr. Crossman?

CROSSMAN. (*Pleasantly.*) You're making it a little harder than usual: is who fascinating?

ROSE. Nicholas Denery, of course.

CROSSMAN. Of course. I don't know. (*Rises, crosses* U. *to door.*)

ROSE. But, goodness. Didn't you all grow up together? (*Crosses to telephone chair.*) I mean you and Constance and Mrs. Ellis and ——

CROSSMAN. (*In door.*) I don't remember any of us as fascinating. Do you, Carrie? (CARRIE *shakes her head, laughs as* SOPHIE, *carrying tray with brandy and brandy glasses, comes into the room. She is followed by* LEON, *a young, colored butler, carrying coffee and demi-tasse cups.* LEON *puts coffee on table* U. R., *serves* MRS. ELLIS *and* CARRIE. FREDERICK *rises and takes tray from* SOPHIE. *She looks at him and smiles.* FREDERICK *puts brandy on table.*)

ROSE. (*Crossing* R. *to* SOPHIE.) Let's see your party dress, Sophie. (SOPHIE *at* U. C. FREDERICK *crosses* D. R. SOPHIE *smiles shyly, takes off her apron, holds it in her hand.*) Oh. It's right nice. But you should wear fluffier things, dear. (LEON *serves coffee to* MRS. ELLIS *and* CARRIE, *then exits into hall.*) Most European girls have such chic —— (GENERAL GRIGGS *gets up, as if he were annoyed, crosses* L. *to door.*) They have, Ben. You said it yourself when you came back from the Pacific.

MRS. ELLIS. Pacific? I thought you fought in Europe?

GRIGGS. I did. Robert Taylor fought in the Pacific. (SOPHIE *crosses* U. R., *puts apron on tray.* GENERAL GRIGGS *wanders off to porch, sits* R. *chair on porch. After his speech the phone rings.* FREDERICK *starts for door as if he already knew it was for him. At the same time* CONSTANCE TUCKERMAN *comes through hall. She is a handsome woman of forty-three or forty-four, usually calm and dignified. Now she is nervous. She is carrying a flower vase.*)

CONSTANCE. Yes. Just a minute, Frederick. Mr. Payson would like to speak to you. (*She crosses* D. *to* L. *of table.* FREDERICK *immediately and swiftly moves to phone, takes it into hall.*) Sorry coffee was late. You all want more just ring. And do, Carrie, explain to the Carters why I can't come to their party this year ——

10

ROSE. (*Crossing* D. *to above sofa.*) Any news from them, Constance?

CONSTANCE. (*Looking at flowers she is carrying.*) News from whom?

ROSE. (*Laughs.*) Oh, come now. Stop pretending. When do the Denerys arrive? (CROSSMAN *puts cup down on tray* U. R.)

CONSTANCE. (*Deliberately.*) Don't wait up for them, Rose. You'll see them at breakfast. (*She turns, goes out and goes up the stairs.* SOPHIE *crosses* L. *with two cups of coffee.* SOPHIE *gives* ROSE *coffee.* ROSE *crosses* D., *sits* R. *end of sofa.* CROSSMAN *crosses* D. R. *to above table, gets brandy and two glasses.* SOPHIE *crosses to porch, gives* GRIGGS *coffee.*)

ROSE. My, Constance is nervous. Well, I suppose I should be if I were seeing an *old beau* for the first time—but I don't believe in old beaus. Beaus should be *brand new*, or just friends, don't you think? (CROSSMAN *starts* L., *stops* C. SOPHIE *crosses into room to above chair* L. *of sofa.* CROSSMAN *starts out to porch, carrying his coffee and brandy bottle.* ROSE *points outside, meaning* GENERAL GRIGGS *and* CROSSMAN.) Now are you boys just going to sit there and share that bottle ——?

CROSSMAN. (*At* R. *of* U. *table on porch.*) General Griggs is only being kind when he says he shares this bottle with me. (*Puts brandy on upper table on porch, fixes drinks, crosses* D., *sits* L. *chair on porch.* FREDERICK *comes in, starts to speak, changes his mind, crosses to above table.*)

CARRIE. (*Carefully.*) Was that Mr. Payson on the phone?

FREDERICK. Yes.

CARRIE. Is he coming to the party?

FREDERICK. No. How many generations do you have to summer in this joint before you're invited to the Carters'? (SOPHIE *crosses to* U. R., *gets coffee.*)

MRS. ELLIS. Oh, that's not true. They're very liberal lately. (*Points to* MRS. GRIGGS. SOPHIE *crosses* D. R. *with coffee, sits.*) After all, the last few years they've always included Mrs. Griggs. (*To* ROSE.) And nobody can be more nouveau riche than your family, can they? I mean your brother during the war and all that.

ROSE. (*Giggles.*) My! Everybody is so jealous of *Henry.* (*Rises.*)

MRS. ELLIS. Well, of course we are. I wish we were nouveau riche again.

11

REDERICK. (*At above table. Gently admonishing her.*) All right, ;randma.

OSE. (*Crossing* U., *puts coffee on phone table.*) Oh, I don't mind. enjoy your grandmother. (*Exits upstairs.*)

'REDERICK. (*Smiling, minimizing it. To* CARRIE.) I'm sorry I'm ιot going to be able to take you to the party. I hope you'll xcuse me, Sophie. Mother. Grandma. (SOPHIE *puts her cup on amp table* D. R.)

:ARRIE. (*Carefully.*) What has happened, Frederick?

'REDERICK. Payson had a wire from his publishers. They want he MS in the mail tomorrow morning. (*Goes to take MS from able, from above it.*)

:ARRIE. (*Slowly.*) I don't understand. (*Rises, stage* R.) We're ·eady to *leave*, Frederick.

=REDERICK. (CARRIE *turns* R. *at* D. R. *chair. A little sharp.*) Mother, !'m not going to the party. I wasn't making a joke ——

:ARRIE. (*Crossing* L. *to above* R. *chair.*) Oh, I hoped you were. You have no obligation to us, or Sophie? An appointment broken, because Payson summons you?

FREDERICK. I am sorry, Sophie. Maybe I can pick you up later. (*Haltingly.*) I *am* sorry.

SOPHIE. (*Rising.*) I do not mind, really. It is better this way.

CARRIE. Don't you? Why not? (*No answer.*) Why don't you mind, Sophie?

SOPHIE. (*Smiles.*) I do not like parties. I did not want to go. Now Frederick has some important business and must leave quickly ——

CARRIE. Perhaps you are going to make *too* good a wife. (SOPHIE *sits* D. R.)

FREDERICK. (*Not sharp.*) Suppose you let me decide that, Mother. (*With finality.*) Good night. Have a good time. See you in the morning —— (*Starts up.*)

CARRIE. (*Crossing to above table. Slight plea.*) I want to talk to you, Frederick.

FREDERICK. (*Stops, smiles. Crosses* D. *to* U. R. *of sofa.*) Let's make it in the morning, Mother.

CARRIE. I ask you to break your appointment with Payson. As a favor to me.

FREDERICK. There's nothing important about my being at the party, and it is important to him. He wants to consult me ——

CARRIE. (*Sharply.*) He is always consulting you. You talk like a

12

public accountant or a landscape gardener. Why should he want to consult *you* about his work?

FREDERICK. (*Hurt.*) Maybe because I try to write and maybe because he thinks I know a little. I realize that's hard for you to believe ——

CARRIE. (*Impatient.*) I didn't mean that. (FREDERICK *stops* U. R. *of sofa. Crosses* L. *to him.*) I am getting tired of Mr. Payson, Frederick. When he came to stay with us in town last winter, I fully understood that he was a brilliant and gifted man and I was glad for you to have such a friend. But when he followed you down here this summer ——

FREDERICK. (*Angrily, but quietly. Trying to control his anger.*) He did not follow me down here, and I wouldn't like you to put it that way again. He came here for the summer and is that your business, Mother?

CARRIE. (*Nervously.*) There is just too much of Mr. Payson. Every day or every evening —— How often do you take Sophie with you? (*Sharply.*) How often have you seen Mr. Payson this summer, Sophie? (SOPHIE *turns to her. No answer.*) Please answer me.

FREDERICK. And please stop using that tone to Sophie. Say what you have to say to me.

CARRIE. (*Crossing* R. *to* L. *of* MRS. ELLIS. *Turning and appealing to* MRS. ELLIS, *who has been watching them.*) Mother, please tell Frederick. (FREDERICK *crosses* L. *to above* C. *of sofa.*)

MRS. ELLIS. I've been dozing. How many hours have passed?

CARRIE. (*Slowly.*) You are always dozing when there is something unpleasant to face out with Frederick.

MRS. ELLIS. What better time? You all want to know something's been worrying me all day? Nobody in the South has tapeworm any more. (CARRIE *crosses few steps* R. *to above table. Rises, crosses to* U. R. *of sofa.*) In my day that was all you ever heard. Tapeworm, tapeworm, tapeworm. (*Looks at* CARRIE.) Now kiss your mother good-night, boy. Otherwise she'll be most unhappy. And say you forgive her. (*Starts up.*)

FREDERICK. (MRS. ELLIS *stops* U. C.) I have nothing to forgive her for, Grandma.

MRS. ELLIS. Of course not. But even when your mother starts out being right she talks and talks until she gets around to being wrong. (*Exits* U. R. *There is silence.*)

CARRIE. (Softly, crossing L. few steps to C.) I'm sorry if I spoke unfairly, or at the wrong time ——
FREDERICK. (Crossing R. to her. Comes to her, smiling. As to a child.) You didn't, you didn't. Now don't feel bad. Nothing's happened. And don't let Grandma tease you.
CARRIE. I know. (She turns to go.) You go ahead, dear. (He kisses her.) Try to join us later. (She smiles, pleased, goes out U. R. FREDERICK stands thinking, then turns to SOPHIE. SOPHIE picks up cup. Rises, crosses to below chair R. of table, puts cup on table.)
FREDERICK. (Crossing D. to U. L. of table.) Sophie, Mother didn't mean to be sharp with you. But when she is, you mustn't let her. She's a little bossy from time to time, but no harm in it. You look so worried.
SOPHIE. (Very puzzled.) Your mother is not angry now?
FREDERICK. Of course not. You mustn't take these things too seriously. Mother is like that.
SOPHIE. (Smiles.) You know it is most difficult in another language. Everything in English sounds so important. I get a headache from the strain of listening.
FREDERICK. (Laughs.) Don't. It's not worth it. (Crosses D. to D. L. of table. Looks at her, then slowly.) Mother is right: I have been rude and neglectful. But I haven't meant to be, Sophie.
SOPHIE. No, no. You have not been.
FREDERICK. And in two weeks Mother and I will be going off to Europe. I hope you don't mind about the European trip. It was all arranged long before you and I—(Stares at her, smiles.) got engaged. (She smiles at him as if she were embarrassed.) We're an awkward pair. I like you, Sophie.
SOPHIE. (Warmly.) I like you, Frederick.
FREDERICK. (Encouraged.) Sophie, I think we'll have to sit down soon and talk about ourselves. I don't think we even know how we got engaged. We haven't said much of anything ——
SOPHIE. (Crossing L. to R. of coffee table.) Sometimes it is better not to say things. There is time, and things will come as they come.
FREDERICK. (Crossing L. to her.) The day we got engaged we tried to speak as honestly as we both knew how, but we didn't say very much ——
SOPHIE. And I think we should not try so hard to talk. It will come better if we give it time.

14

FREDERICK. We *will* give it time. And you'll make no decisions and set no dates until you are sure about what you think and feel.
SOPHIE. (*Definitely.*) Oh, I have made the decision for myself. And I am pleased.
FREDERICK. (*Pleased.*) And you are quite sure of your decision?
SOPHIE. You know, sometimes I think all of you make decisions only in order to speak about them.
FREDERICK. (*Appreciating her intelligence.*) Yes. We'll get along fine. I want you to know that I feel very lucky.
SOPHIE. (*Crossing* L. *to below coffee table.*) You will have to be patient with me. I am not a good success here.
FREDERICK. (*Crossing* L. *to her.*) Now, you stop that. I don't want you a good success. And you're to stop thinking it. You're to stop a lot of things: letting Mother boss you about, letting Mrs. Griggs tell you what to wear ——
SOPHIE. Oh, I do not mind. Because I look so bad makes Mrs. Griggs think she looks so good. (*Laughs.*)
FREDERICK. (*Smiles.*) Good night, my dear. (*Touches her arm.*)
SOPHIE. (*Smiles.*) Good night. (*He exits* U. L. SOPHIE *crosses* U. *to above table, puts cups and glasses on tray.* ROSE GRIGGS *comes down the steps carrying a little evening bag. She comes into the room.*)
ROSE. (*Crossing to* C.) Where are the Ellises?
SOPHIE. They went to the party, Mrs. Griggs. (*Picks up brandy tray, exits up.*)
ROSE. (*Crossing* L. *to bookcase.*) No! Without me? I *must* say that's very rude. (*Goes to porch door.*) Ben. (*He looks up.*) The Ellises left without me, Ben!
GRIGGS. Yes?
ROSE. (*Piqued.*) You'll have to walk me over. I just won't go in alone.
GRIGGS. (*Puts book on table. Not annoyed.*) It's across the street, Rose. Not a very dangerous journey. (*Rises, crosses in to above* L. *of sofa.*)
ROSE. (*Gently.*) Ben. (*Backs* R. *a few steps. Crosses* L. *to him.*) You know, I think it's shocking. In front of other people. God knows what they know or guess this summer. (*Crosses to* U. C. *Flirting.*) You won't even walk over with me?
GRIGGS. (*Crossing* R. *a step to above* C. *of sofa.*) Certainly I will.

ROSE. (*Smiles.*) No, you don't have to. I just wanted to see if you would. Will you call for me, at *twelve*, say?

GRIGGS. (*Wearily.*) What mischief is this, Rose?

ROSE. Is it mischief to want to talk with you?

GRIGGS. (*Crossing* L. *to chair* L. *of sofa. Forbearing.*) Again? To-night? And every night and every day? The same things over and over? We're worn out, Rose, both of us. (*Kindly.*) There *is* no more to say. (*Sits.*)

ROSE. (*Softly.*) No more to say. (*Crosses* D. *and* L., *sits sofa above coffee table.*) Do people get divorces, after twenty-five years, by just saying they want them and that's all, and walking off?

GRIGGS. (*Tenderly.*) I suppose some men do. But I haven't walked off, and I have said all I know how to say.

ROSE. But you haven't really explained *anything* to me. You tell me that you want a divorce —— And I ask why, why, why? We've been happy together.

GRIGGS. You don't believe that.

ROSE. When people get our age, well, the worst is over and what else can one do? (*Exasperated.*) I never really heard of such a thing. I'm just not taking you seriously and I do wish you'd stop talking about it. (*Rises, crosses* R. *to* R. *of sofa. Turns back. After a pause.*) You've never given me a good reason. I ask you ten times a day if there's another woman. I could understand that. Of course you say no, naturally ——

GRIGGS. (*Rises, crossing around to behind his chair. Easily.*) There is no other woman.

ROSE. (*Crossing* L. *above sofa. Giggles.*) You know what I think? I think it's that little blonde at the drug store, and the minute my back is turned ——

GRIGGS. (*Slightly irritated.*) Please, Rose. Please stop talking like that.

ROSE. Never at any time, during this divorce talk, have you mentioned them. (*Crosses* R. *to above chair* L. *of table.*) You'd think we didn't have sons. It will break their hearts.

GRIGGS. (*Sits on arm of sofa at* L. *end. Matter-of-fact.*) Their hearts won't be broken.

ROSE. (*Softly, shocked.*) You can't love them, to speak that way.

GRIGGS. (*Emphatically.*) I don't love them. I did love them, but I don't now. They're hard men to love.

16

ROSE. (*Exasperated.*) Oh, I don't believe a word you say. You've always enjoyed shocking me. (*Crosses* L. *to* R. *of sofa.*) You've been a wonderful father and you're just as devoted to them as they are to you.

GRIGGS. They aren't the least devoted to me—when they think about me it is to find my name useful, and when it isn't useful they disapprove of me.

ROSE. Look, Ben. I'm late now. I just can't stay and talk all night. There's no use our saying the same things over and over again —— (*Crosses* U. *few steps. Turns back.*) If you won't come to the party what are you going to do?

GRIGGS. (*Smiles.*) I am going down by the water, sit on a bench and study from a Chinese grammar.

ROSE. You'll be lonely.

GRIGGS. (*Smiles.*) Yes, but not for parties.

ROSE. It's very hard to take seriously a man who spends the evening with a Chinese grammar. I'll never forget that winter with the Hebrew phonograph records. Now, good night, darling. And don't worry about me: I am going to try to have a good time. We'll talk about all this another day. (*Starts upstage.*)

GRIGGS. (*Rises, crossing* R. *above sofa to* U. R. *of sofa.*) No. No, we're not going to do that. You're turning it into a pleasure, Rose, something to chatter about. I've told you it isn't going to be that way. (*She is in hall.*) It isn't going to be that way. When you go back to town next week I'm not going with you. (CROSSMAN *looks toward sound of their voices.* ROSE *crosses* U. *slowly.*)

ROSE'S VOICE. (*From hall.*) Good night, darling. (*Exits* U. R.)

GRIGGS. (*Stands still for a moment. Then turns, sees his book on porch table. Goes out to porch, realizes doors have been open. Leans against pillar. To* CROSSMAN.) I guess we thought the doors were closed. I am sorry.

CROSSMAN. (*Smiles.*) Don't be. (GRIGGS *crosses* D., *looking at* CROSSMAN.)

GRIGGS. (R. *of* R. *chair.*) You know, Ned, there are so many things I want to do that I don't know which to do first. Have you ever thought about starting a new life?

CROSSMAN. I've often thought that if I started all over again, I'd go right back to where I started and start from there.

GRIGGS. Where did you start from?

17

CROSSMAN. (*Smiles. Nods.*) Nowhere. That's the trouble. (*Puts paper on table.*)

GRIGGS. (*Leaning back. Recalling.* CROSSMAN *sips drink.*) I started with mathematics. Seems strange now, but that's why I went to West Point—wonderful mathematics department there. So I got myself two wars instead. (*Leans forward.*) I'm going somewhere now and study for a few years, or —— (*Smiles.*) Anyway, sit down by myself and—(*Closing fist.*) think.

CROSSMAN. Europe?

GRIGGS. (*Planning.*) I don't think so. Europe seemed like a tourist joint the last time. I don't want sentimental journeys to old battlefields. I'll start tame enough: I've written my sister that I'd like to stay with her for a month or two.

CROSSMAN. Isn't that a sentimental journey?

GRIGGS. (*Smiles, agreeing.*) I suppose it is. I really want to see her because she looks like my mother. The last six months I've thought a lot about my mother. If I could just go back to her for a day. Crazy at my age ——

CROSSMAN. I know. We all do at times. Age has nothing to do with it. It's when we're in trouble.

GRIGGS. (*Rises, to above table.*) I don't know why I want to say this but, well, don't think too badly of my wife.

CROSSMAN. (*Rather bitterly.*) Why should I think badly of anybody?

GRIGGS. (*As be turns to go.*) All professional soldiers marry Rose. It's in the Army Manual. She is as she always was. It is my fault, not hers.

CROSSMAN. (*Sarcastically.*) Haven't you lived in the South long enough to know that nothing is *ever* anybody's fault? (*Rises, crosses* U. *to other table on porch, pours drink.* GENERAL GRIGGS *laughs, touches his shoulder, starts out as* CONSTANCE *comes down stairs.* CONSTANCE *has on a different dress and is buttoning belt as she comes into the room.* GENERAL GRIGGS *picks up book and exits stage* L. CONSTANCE *looks around, picks up cup from phone table, puts it on butler's tray. Puts cigarettes from table* R. C. *to* D. R., *straightens chairs, finds the room is neat, goes out to porch, talking as she goes.*)

CONSTANCE. (*Crossing* D. L. *to* D. L. *chair. Nervously—wondering if everything is done.*) I think everything is ready. I've put Nick in Sophie's room—Sophie says she doesn't mind sleeping down

18

here. Anyway it happens every summer. (CROSSMAN *crosses* D. *to*
R. *chair.*) And I've given Mrs. Denery the yellow room. They
wanted *two* rooms, Nick said on the phone.
CROSSMAN. Fashionable people don't sleep together, don't you
know that? It's not sanitary.
CONSTANCE. (*Sits down on* D. L. *porch chair.*) I'm tired, Ned.
CROSSMAN. Have a brandy.
CONSTANCE. (*Smiling. Nervously.*) No. It would make me nervous.
CROSSMAN. Remarkable the things that make people nervous:
coffee, brandy, relatives, (*Sits* R. *porch chair.*) running water, too
much sun, too little sun. Never anything in themselves, eh,
Constance?
CONSTANCE. (*Not having listened to him.*) They have a maid and
a chauffeur. I'll have to put them in the boathouse. It's all so
much work at the end of the season. Sophie's been cleaning all
day, and I've been cooking —— Why did I say they could come?
CROSSMAN. (*Smiles.*) I wonder why.
CONSTANCE. Well, of *course,* I want to see Nick again. But I am
nervous about meeting her. (*Hesitantly. Points to his glass.*) Do
you think perhaps a sip?
CROSSMAN. Only drunkards borrow other people's drinks. Have
one of your own. (*Gives her his glass. She sips it.*)
CONSTANCE. And I've stuffed some crabs and there's white
wine —— (*Girlish.*) Remember how Nick loved stuffed crabs?
CROSSMAN. (*Smiles.*) No. I don't remember how Nick loved
stuffed crabs.
CONSTANCE. It was twenty-three years ago, the 18th of next
month. I mean the night he decided to go to Paris to study. (*Proud
of* NICK.) Not so many young men from New Orleans went to
Paris in those days.
CROSSMAN. Just as many young men met rich young ladies on
boats.
CONSTANCE. (*Quiet but firm.*) He fell in love. People can't be
blamed for changing their hearts—it just happens. They've had a
fine marriage, and *that's* given me happiness all these years.
CROSSMAN. (*Rises, crossing* R. *around to above his chair. Kidding
her.*) How do you know they've had a "fine" marriage?
CONSTANCE. (*Smiles.*) I know.
CROSSMAN. The rest of us don't know anything about any mar-

riage—but you know all about one you've never seen. You're very wise, Constance. It must come from not thinking.

CONSTANCE. (*Rises. Puts glass down on table. Pause. Smiling.*) Is this dress all right?

CROSSMAN. (*Crossing to above table.*) You've changed your dress three times tonight.

CONSTANCE. My dresses are all so sort of —— Mrs. Denery'll think they're cheap. (*Smiles.*) Well, and so they are. (*There is silence. Then.*) Have we changed much, Ned?

CROSSMAN. (*Kindly but truthful.*) Yes, my dear. You've changed, I've changed. But you're still handsome, if that's what you mean. (*Crosses U. to brandy on table.*)

CONSTANCE. (*Kindly.*) Ned, you don't look well this summer. (*Points to bottle.*) I wanted to tell you —— Don't you think ——?

CROSSMAN. (*Crossing D. to R. of R. chair. Very pleasantly.*) Don't I think you should mind your business? Yes, I do. (SOPHIE *enters from U. L. of porch, comes in, carrying sheets, a quilt, a pillow, puts them down on chair above upstage porch table.*)

CONSTANCE. (*Hurt.*) Isn't what happens to you my business?

SOPHIE. (*Crossing D. to above little porch table.*) You look pretty, Aunt Constance.

CONSTANCE. (*Complimenting* SOPHIE. *To* CROSSMAN.) Sophie made this dress for me. Last winter. What could the girls at school have thought? Sophie sitting sewing for an old country aunt when she could have been out dancing ——?

SOPHIE. (*Practically.*) I sew better than I dance. (*Automobile horn off.* CONSTANCE *crosses into living-room. Then turns, crossing out* U. L. CROSSMAN *has crossed* L. *to* L. *chair, turned to stare at her.* SOPHIE *crosses* U. *few steps, looking after her, at above* R. *chair. Timidly, pointing out toward living-room.*) Should I— should I stay, Mr. Ned?

CROSSMAN. (*At* L. *of* R. *chair. Looking* U. *after* CONSTANCE.) I don't know the etiquette of such meetings.

SOPHIE. Why is Aunt Constance so nervous about the visit of this lady and gentleman?

CROSSMAN. Because she was once in love with Nicholas Denery, this gentleman.

SOPHIE. (*To him.*) Oh. Such a long, long time to stay nervous. (*Slight pause. Sententious.*) Great love in tender nature. And things of such kind. (*As he turns to stare at her.*) It always happens that way with ladies. For them it is once and not again: it is their good breeding that makes it so.

CROSSMAN. What is the matter with you?

SOPHIE. I try very hard to sound nice. I try too hard, perhaps? *(She runs out, exits through L. porch.)*

NICK'S VOICE. *(Off.)* Constance! *(NICK DENERY appears in hall and comes into room. He is about forty-five, handsome, a little soft-looking, and in a few years will be too heavy. He is followed by NINA DENERY, who is a woman of about forty, good-looking, chic, tired and delicate. She stops and stands in doorway. She has her jacket around her shoulders.)*

NICK. *(Calling upstairs.)* Constance! *(Crosses L. above sofa to porch door. NINA stops L. of hall door. NICK and NINA are followed by a maid, HILDA, who stands waiting in hall. She is carrying jewelry case, overnight bag, and two coats. CROSSMAN starts to come forward, changes his mind, draws back, crossing D. L.)*

HILDA. *(At R. in hall door. In German.)* Where shall I take the bags, Madame? [*Wo soll ich das gepaeck hinträgen?*]

NINA. *(In German.)* I don't know. I don't know the house. [*Ich weiss nicht. Ich kenne das Haus nicht.*]

NICK. *Ich weiss* [*es*]. *(Crosses to above sofa. Boasting.)* I know every inch of it. *(Examining the room.)* It was the great summer mansion and as kids we were here more than we were at home —— *(Softly, almost to himself. Crossing to U. L. of sofa.)* The great summer mansion! Did the house change, or me? *(Sees NINA in doorway.)* Come on in.

NINA. *(Crossing in to below phone table. A little nervous.)* Perhaps it would be pleasanter for you to see old friends without me? In any case, I am very tired —— *(Takes jacket off shoulders. CROSSMAN crosses U. to living-room door, watches them.)*

NICK. *(Crossing R. to NINA, takes her arm.)* Oh, now don't get tired. We've just come. Do you realize how often these days you're tired?

NINA. I realize it very well. And I know it bores you.

NICK. It *worries* me. *(Turns toward porch. NINA crosses R. to above L. of table.)* Could you tell me where we could find Miss Tuckerman? *(CROSSMAN has turned and starts L., realizing he has been seen, now comes forward.)*

CROSSMAN. *(Crossing R. to U. L. of sofa.)* Hello, Nick. Good to see you. *(Puts out hand.)*

NICK. (*Crossing to* CROSSMAN. *After a second.*) My God, Willy Crossman! (*They shake hands.*) How many years, how many years? (*Puts his arm around* CROSSMAN, *embraces him.*) Nina, this may be my oldest and best friend in the world. Nina, tell Willy how often I've talked about him and what I said.

CROSSMAN. (*Crossing* R. *to* NINA, *who extends hand. Shaking hands with* NINA. *Amused.*) Mrs. Denery. Then I hope he told you that my name is Edward Crossman, not Willy.

NINA. (*Amused.*) I hope so—but I am not sure.

NICK. (*Crossing* R. *to above sofa. Slightly flustered.*) Your mother always called you Willy. Don't you remember?

CROSSMAN. (*Goes out into hall.*) No. I thought it was my brother's name. (*Crossing* U. NINA *crosses* R. *above to* R. *of table. Calls out, loudly.*) Constance! Nick is here.

NICK. Tell me before I see her. What has happened here? I don't know anything.

CROSSMAN. (*Crossing* D. *to* U. C.) There's very little to know. Old man Tuckerman surprised everybody by dying broke. Constance sold the New Orleans house and managed to hang on to this by turning it into what is called a summer guest house. That's about all, Nick.

NICK. (*Above* U. R. *of sofa.*) Where is Mrs. Tuckerman? I was crazy about her, Nina: she had style.

CROSSMAN. (*Crossing* R. *to above table. Smiling wanly.*) She died shortly after Mr. Tuckerman—just to show him anybody could do it.

NICK. (*Crossing* L. *to* CROSSMAN, *laughs, pats him.*) Good to see you, boy. (*Crosses* R. *to above sofa.*) You know, if anybody had asked me, I would have said this room was as large as an 18th Century ballroom, and as elegant. I think it shrank. All the fine things were sold?

CROSSMAN. The size hasn't changed. And nothing was sold.

NICK. (*Smiles, bewildered.*) Could I have been so wrong all these years? Seems so shabby now and ——

NINA. (*Above* R. *of chair* R. *of table. Quickly, to* CROSSMAN.) I think it is a pleasant room.

NICK. Does Sam live here? (NINA *crosses to* R. *of chair* R. *of table.*)

CROSSMAN. Sam died during the war. He went to Europe—oh, in the 30's, married there and never came back. You'll meet his daughter. Constance imported her five years ago.

22

NICK. (*To* NINA.) And Constance sacrificed her life for her brother.

CROSSMAN. (*To* NINA.) Nick is *still* a Southerner. With us every well-born lady sacrifices her life for something: a man, a house, sometimes a gardenia bush. Is it the same where you come from? (*Crosses* R. *to* NINA.)

NINA. (*Smiles.*) Boston is too cold for gardenias. (*Through* CROSSMAN'S *speech,* CONSTANCE *appears in hall. She moves into room, takes a step toward* NINA, *then turns to* NICK, *smiles nervously and waits for* NICK *to come to her. He takes her face in his hands, kisses her cheek. Then he stands back to look at her.*)

NICK. (*At* U. C.) This is a good hour of my life, Constance.

CONSTANCE. (*Softly.*) And of mine.

NICK. (*Holds her shoulders.*) You've changed and you've changed well.

CONSTANCE. (*Crossing* D. *to below table. Remembers* NINA, *becomes confused, moves away from him, comes to* NINA. NICK *crosses to* D. R. *of sofa.*) Forgive me, Mrs. Denery.

NINA. (*Crosses to below chair* R. *of table. Puts out her hand, warmly.*) Hello.

CONSTANCE. (*Flossy.*) I should have been here to make you as welcome as you truly are. I was reading when you arrived, reading a book, and I didn't hear the car. (*She sees* CROSSMAN *is staring at her and she looks nervously away from him.* CROSSMAN *crosses* L. *above sofa to* D. L. *of chair* L. *of sofa.*)

NICK. I had expected you standing in the driveway with the sun in your face, in the kind of lovely pink thing you used to wear——

NINA. (*Lightly.*) The sun is not usually out at night—even for you.

NICK. (*To* CONSTANCE.) Instead, you are reading, (CONSTANCE *looks at* CROSSMAN, *who is staring at her*) as if you were waiting for the groceries to come.

CONSTANCE. (*Crossing* U. *to* NICK. *Quickly.*) I wasn't reading. It was a silly lie. I was just pretending —— (*Embarrassed.*) Well, I'm even forgetting my manners. (*Crosses toward* NINA.) You must be hungry, Mrs. Denery, and I've got ——

NICK. (*Laughs, takes her shoulders, moves her toward couch. She sits.*) No, no. Stop your manners, girl. There's a great deal I want to know. (CROSSMAN *crosses to behind chair* L. *of sofa. They sit*

23

*down,* NICK *on end,* CONSTANCE *in* C. *of sofa.* NINA *sits* R. *of table.*) Now, do you still have the portrait?

CONSTANCE. Still have the portrait! It's the only important thing I have got.

NICK. Is it as good as I remember it? (*At* NINA.) I want Nina to see it. Nina knows a great deal about painting. Sometimes I think she knows more than I.

CONSTANCE. (*Smiles to* NINA, *nods. Then to* NICK.) You know, Nick, I subscribe to the New York Sunday Times. Because of the art section. I wanted to follow your career.

NICK. (*Carefully.*) You haven't often found me in the Times. I've only exhibited in Europe.

CONSTANCE. (*Relieved. Looks at* CROSSMAN.) Oh. That explains it. (*To* NINA.) I like painting. I like Renoir best. (*To* CROSSMAN.) The summer ladies in the gardens, so very, very pretty, I think.

NICK. (*Rises, crossing* R. *to above chair* L. *of table.*) Yes, very pretty.—This is the same wonderful place —— My God, we had happy summers here, all of us! We loved each other so very much. Remember, Ned?

CROSSMAN. (*Lightly.*) I don't remember that much love.

NINA. (*Laughs.*) I like you, Mr. Crossman.

NICK. (*Crossing* R. *to above* NINA, *puts arm round her shoulder. Sincerely, quieter.*) Of course you like him. These are my oldest friends. (*Crosses* L. *to* C.) I think as one grows older it is more and more necessary to reach out your hand for the sturdy old vines you knew when you were young and let them lead you back to the roots of things that matter. (*Crosses* R. *to above table. Turns to* NED *above table.* NINA *clears throat. Even* CONSTANCE *is a little overwhelmed.*) Isn't that true, Ned?

CROSSMAN. I daresay.

NICK. (*Crossing* L. *to* C.) Now what have you been up to all these years?

CROSSMAN. I still work in the bank and come here for my vacation. That's about all.

NICK. (*Not being cruel.*) I bumped into Louis Prescott in Paris a couple of years ago and he told me you and Constance had never married —— (CONSTANCE *looks embarrassed, rises, crosses to* L. *of sofa.*) Couldn't understand it. No wonder you drink too much, Ned.

24

CROSSMAN. (*Crossing* R. *to* U. R. *of sofa. Slight edge.*) Louis Prescott go all the way to Paris to tell you that?
NICK. (*Embarrassed.*) Oh, look, old boy, (NINA *rises, stands* R. *of chair.*) I didn't *mean* anything—I drank too much myself. I only want to know about you and have you know about me. I hope you didn't mind, Ned?
CROSSMAN. (*Smiling.*) Not a bit. I want to know about you, too. Ever had syphilis, Nick? Kind of thing one has to know right off, if you understand me.
CONSTANCE. Ned, how can you speak that way?
NICK. (*Smiles.*) You've grown edgy. I didn't remember you that way.
CROSSMAN. (*Starts up. Pleasantly.*) Oh, I don't think I've changed. See you in the morning.
NICK. (*Crossing* U. *with* CROSSMAN, *who is* R. *of phone table.*) Hope you'll take me around, show me all the old places ——
CROSSMAN. Of course I will. Good night, Mrs. Denery, and welcome to you.
NINA. Good night, Mr. Crossman. (*Crosses* U. *few steps.* CROSSMAN *exits up stair-case.*)
NICK. (*Looks at* NINA, *then speaks. Crosses* R. *few steps. To* CONSTANCE, *meaning* CROSSMAN.) I'm sorry if I said anything ——
CONSTANCE. (*Crossing* R. *above sofa to* U. R. *of sofa.* NINA *crosses to above* R. *chair. Embarrassed.*) You know, for years I've been meeting you and Mrs. Denery—in my mind. I mean—it was so important to me—our first meeting —— (*Sadly.*) And now when it happens ——
NICK. (*At* C. *Heartily.*) Nonsense. My homecoming is just as it should be. We took up right where we left off: even Ned and I. Let us be as we were, my dear, with no years between us, and no pretending.
CONSTANCE. (*Touches his arm. Delighted with him, warmly.*) Thank you. (*Crosses* R. *to above chair* L. *of table. Goes to* NINA.) All these years I wanted to write you. (NICK *wanders* L. *above* C. *of sofa.*) I did write but I never sent the letters. It seemed so intrusive of me. I could see you getting the letter and just not knowing who I was.
NICK. (*Crossing* R. *to her.*) I told Nina about you the first night I met her (NINA *turns away.*) and through the years she has done quite a little teasing —— (NINA *turns to him.*) You are too

25

modest, Constance. (*Suddenly.*) Now are you going to let me do another portrait of you?

CONSTANCE. (*Looks at* NINA. *Laughs.*) Another portrait? No, no, indeed. I want to remember myself as I was in the picture upstairs.

NICK. Go and get it for me. I want to look at it with you. (*She smiles, exits. There is silence.* NICK *crosses* U. *after her.* NINA *crosses* L. *above to above sofa.* NICK *crosses* D. *to* U. C.) You haven't been too warm or gracious, Nina.

NINA. (*Lightly.*) What can I do when I don't even know the plot?

NICK. What are you talking about?

NINA. (*Crossing* R. *few steps. Quizzing him.*) You told me about Constance Tuckerman the first night we met? And about dear Willy or Ned, and I've done quite a little teasing about her all these years?

NICK. I did tell you about her immediately ——

NINA. You mentioned her very casually, last week, and you said that you could hardly remember anything more about her than a rather silly ——

NICK. (*Crossing* L. *to her. Quickly.*) Are you going to be bad-tempered for our whole visit here? For years I've looked forward to coming back —— (NINA *laughs.*)

NINA. So you came to do her portrait?

NICK. (*Annoyed.*) No, I didn't "come to do it." (*Crosses* R. *few steps.*) I thought about it driving down here. (*Turns back to her.*) If the one I did is as good as I remember it would be wonderful for the show. The *young girl*, the *woman* at forty-five. (*Crosses* R. D.) She's aged. Have we changed that much? I don't think you've changed, darling. (*Sits chair* R. *of table.*)

NINA. (*Crossing* R. *to* L. *of table. Emphatically.*) I've changed a great deal. And I wouldn't want to have it pointed out to me in a portrait to be hung side by side with a picture of what I used to be. (*He doesn't answer her. Hurt.*) That isn't a nice reason for being here, and if I had known it ——

NICK. (*Laughs slightly.*) We have no "reason" for being here. I just wanted to come back. Nothing mysterious about it ——

NINA. (*Reproving him quietly.*) You're simply looking for a new area in which to "exercise" yourself. It has happened many, many times before. But it *always* happens when we return from Europe and spend a month in Boston. It's been too important to you, for many years, that you cannot manage to charm my family. And so, when our visit is finished there, you inevitably look around for —— Well, you know. (*Crosses* u. *Sadly.*) You know what's been, and the *trouble.* (*Turns* u. R. *of sofa.*)

NICK. (*Cheerfully.*) I don't know what the hell you're talking about.

NINA. I'm *tired* of such troubles, Nick ——

NICK. (*Rises, crossing slowly above table to her. Quietly.*) Do you know that these sharp moods of yours grow more sharp with time? Now I would like to have a happy visit here. But if something is disturbing you and you'd prefer not to stay, I'll arrange immediately ——

NINA. (*At above* u. R. *of sofa. As if she were a little frightened that he might send her away.*) I'd only prefer to go to bed. (*Sincerely.*) Sorry if I've been churly about your—home-coming. (NICK *smiles, kisses her, then crosses to* R. *of door. She starts out door, meets* CONSTANCE *who comes in carrying portrait, crosses to* L. *of hall door.*) Will you excuse me, Constance? The long drive gave me a headache.

CONSTANCE. (*At* R. *of* NINA.) I am sorry. Will I bring you a tray upstairs?

NINA. No, thank you. (*Crosses* u. *onto first step.* CONSTANCE *moves as if to show her the way.*)

NICK. (*Anxiously.*) Come on, I want to see the picture. Nina will find her way. (*He takes picture from* CONSTANCE, *crossing* D. *to* R. *of chair* R. *of table.*)

CONSTANCE. The yellow room on the left. Your maid is unpacking. I peeked in. What lovely clothes. Can I come and see them tomorrow?

NINA. (*Going up stairs.*) Yes, of course. Thank you and good night. (CONSTANCE *watches her, then comes into room, crossing* D. *to* L. *of table.*)

NICK. (*Who is looking at picture.*) I was nervous about seeing it. Damn good work for a boy of eighteen.

CONSTANCE. You were twenty-two, Nick.

NICK. No, I wasn't.

CONSTANCE. You finished it the morning of your birthday. (*She points to windows.*) And when you put down your brushes, you said "damn good work for a boy of twenty-two," and then you asked me to marry you. Don't you remember ——? (*Crosses* L.

27

*few steps. She stops, embarrassed.*) Why should you remember? (*Self-reproach.*) And I don't want to talk that way.

NICK. (*Preoccupied with picture.*) Oh, nonsense. Talk any way you like. We were in love, Con, very much in love, and why shouldn't we speak of it?

CONSTANCE. (*Very embarrassed at how much picture means to her.*) After I die, the picture will go to the Delgado Museum.

NICK. (*At R. of table. Laughs.*) I want to borrow it first. I'm having a retrospective show this winter, in London. (*Crosses L. to above table.*) I've done a lot of fancy people in Europe, you know that, but I'll be more proud of this —— (*Puts portrait on table.*) And I want to do another portrait of you as you are now. (*Moves L. toward porch, to above C. of sofa. CONSTANCE crosses u. few steps, excited.*) You standing out there. As before. Wonderful idea; young girl, (*Gestures toward her.*) woman at —— (*Hits fist in hand.*) Be a sensation. Constance, it's fascinating how faces change, (*Crosses R. few steps, looking at her face.*) mold firm or loose, have lines that start in youth and ——

CONSTANCE. (*At u. R. of sofa. Step L. toward him. Very firmly.*) Oh, Nick. I don't want to see myself now. I don't want to see all the changes. And I don't want other people to stand and talk about them. (*Turns away.*) I don't want people to laugh at me or pity me. (*Hurt.*) Oh, Nick!

NICK. (*Touches her shoulder. Laughs.*) I see. (*Turns. Crosses L. to above sofa.*) Well, it would have meant a lot to me. But that's that. (*Starts R.*) I'll be off to bed now ——

CONSTANCE. (*Coming after him. Stops him above sofa.*) But we haven't had a minute. And I have supper all ready for you ——

NICK. (*Crossing R. above her. Cordially.*) Good night, my dear.

CONSTANCE. (*Stops him at her R. Childlike, slowly.*) You think I'm being selfish and vain? I mean, am I the only woman who wouldn't like ——?

NICK. No, I think most women would feel the same way. (*He starts out.*)

CONSTANCE. (*Stops L. of hall door.*) Do you prefer breakfast in bed? And what shall I make for your dinner? Pompano —— (*He is at door as CARRIE and ROSE come into hall. CARRIE has ROSE by the arm.*)

CARRIE. Hello, Nick. (*She comes to door with ROSE on her R.*)

28

NICK. (*At L. of hall door. Takes her hands.*) My God, Carrie! I didn't know you were here. How come? It's wonderful ——

CARRIE. (*Between* ROSE *and* NICK.) We come every summer.

NICK. (*At L. of hall door.*) You're handsome, Carrie. But you always were.

CARRIE. (*Smiles.*) And you always remembered to say so. (ROSE *touches* CARRIE'S *shoulder.*) This is Mrs. Griggs. (*To* CONSTANCE.) Mrs. Griggs didn't feel well, so I brought her home. (*Chiding* ROSE.) She became a little dizzy, dancing.

ROSE. (*Crossing* CARRIE *to* NICK. *To* NICK, *who is shaking hands with her.*) You're a famous gentleman in this town, sir, and I've been looking forward so to seeing you. We lead dull lives here, you know ——

NICK. (*Laughs.*) *You* don't look as if you do.

ROSE. Oh, thank you. But I don't look well tonight. (*Recalling the moment.*) I became suddenly a little ill ——

CARRIE. (*Pokes her R. arm, crossing above and to L. of ROSE. Tartly.*) Yes. Well, come along. If you still feel ill. (*They move to stairs.*)

NICK. (*Crossing R., takes her R. arm.*) Can I help you, Mrs. Griggs?

ROSE. (*Crossing D. to* NICK'S L. *Delighted.*) Oh, thank you. That would be nice. I haven't been well this summer —— (NICK *starts into hall.*)

CONSTANCE. (*At below phone table chair.*) Nick —— (*He pays no attention.* CARRIE *takes* ROSE'S L. *arm.*)

CARRIE. (*Not taking* ROSE *seriously.*) Come on, Mrs. Griggs. Good night, Nick. I look forward to seeing you in the morning. Hope you're staying for a while.

NICK. I think we'll have to leave tomorrow.

ROSE. (*Crossing D. a step.*) Oh, don't do that. (*Then.*) Constance, if Ben comes in would you tell him I was taken ill? (CARRIE *impatiently pushes her ahead and up steps, past* NICK, *who steps upstage.*)

NICK. Good night.

ROSE. Good night.

NICK. Good night, Carrie.

CARRIE. Good night, Nick.

NICK. (*Meaning* ROSE.) Pretty woman, that Mrs. Griggs, or was. (*Looks at* CONSTANCE.) What is it, Con? (*In hall door.*)

29

CONSTANCE. How can you talk of leaving tomorrow? (*He doesn't answer.*) Don't be mad with me, Nick.

NICK. I don't get mad, darling.

CONSTANCE. (*Her voice stops him as he is about to leave. Catches him as he is almost out the door.*) Please, Nick, please let me change my mind. (*Crosses to* R. *of table.*) You are welcome to take this picture, and I am flattered you wish to do another. (NICK *crosses* D.) But I'll have to pose early, before they're all down for breakfast ——

NICK. (*Turns, crossing* D. *to* D. R. *of sofa. Pleased.*) Good. We'll start in the morning. (*With friendly enthusiasm.*) Do you make a living out of this place, darling?

CONSTANCE. (*Making conversation. Gaily.*) Not much of one. (*Sits* R. *of table, puts hands on table.* NICK *crosses, sits* L. *of table.*) The last few years have been a little hard. I brought Sam's daughter from Europe—she and her mother went through the occupation and were very poor—(NICK *puts his hand over hers.*) and I've tried to send her to the best school, and then she was to make her debut, only now she wants to get married, I think, and ——

NICK. (*Sympathetic.*) The girl expected all that from you ——

CONSTANCE. Oh, no. (*She becomes aware of* NICK'S *hand. Embarrassed, withdraws it.* NICK *leans back in chair, scratches neck.*) Her mother didn't want to come and Sophie didn't want to leave her mother. I finally had really to *demand* that Sam's daughter was not to grow up —— Well, I just can't describe it. At thirteen she was working in a fish store or whatever you call it over there. I just *made* her come over ——

NICK. Why didn't you ever marry Ned? (CONSTANCE *starts to answer, doesn't.*)

CONSTANCE. (*Turns slightly* R.) I can't answer such questions, Nick. Even for you.

NICK. Why not? I'd tell you about myself or Nina.

CONSTANCE. Oh, it's one thing to talk about lives that have been good and full and happy, and quite another—I don't know. (*Turns away.* NICK *rises.*) We just never did marry . . .

NICK. (*Crossing* U. *to above chair* L. *of table.*) Well, then, tomorrow morning. (SOPHIE *enters from upstage of porch with pajamas and robe, gets sheets, pillow from chair.*) I'll do a good portrait of you because it's the face of a *good* woman —— (*He*

30

stops as SOPHIE *comes in from porch with pajamas and robe and bed clothes. She sees* NICK *and* CONSTANCE, *draws back a little.*)
SOPHIE. I'm sorry.
CONSTANCE. Sophie. (*Rises.* SOPHIE *comes into room.*) This is Sam's daughter. (NICK *crosses* L. *to her at above sofa.*)
NICK. (*Very warmly, to* SOPHIE.) I've been looking forward to meeting you for many years. (CONSTANCE *crosses to above table, puzzled.*)
CONSTANCE. Looking forward?
SOPHIE. How do you do, sir?
NICK. You follow in the great tradition of Tuckerman good looks. (GRIGGS *enters from doors* D. R., *crosses to above chair* R. *of table.*)
SOPHIE. Er—Er ——
CONSTANCE. (*Crossing* U. *few steps. Smiles.*) Don't er, dear. Say thank you. (*Turns* R. *Sees* GRIGGS. SOPHIE *crosses* D., *puts bedclothes, etc. on chair* L. *of sofa, then turns out porch light.*) Do come in. (GRIGGS *comes in.*) This is General Griggs. My very old friend Nicholas Denery. (*They meet* C.)
GRIGGS. How do you do.
NICK. (*Expansive.*) Are you General Benjamin Griggs, sir? I've read about you in Raymond's book, and Powell's.
GRIGGS. (*As they shake hands.*) I hear they disagree about me.
NICK. (*At* L. *of* GRIGGS.) We almost met before this. When your boys marched into Paris. I was in France during the German occupation.
GRIGGS. *That* must have been unpleasant for you.
NICK. Yes, it was. But in the end, one has to be just; the Germans were damn smart about the French. They acted like gentlemen.
GRIGGS. (*Crossing* L. *past* NICK. *Pleasantly.*) That's a side of them I didn't see. (*Looks over at* SOPHIE.) You didn't either, Sophie? (*Crosses* L. *to* D. S. *pillar.* SOPHIE *crosses* L. *to chair to get sheet. During his speech* HILDA, *the maid, appears in doorway from stairs.*)
HILDA. (*Crossing to a step below* C. *of door. In German.*) [Excuse me, Mr. Denery. Mrs. Denery would like you to come for a minute. She has a little surprise gift she bought for you in New Orleans.] [(*German:*) Entschuldigen Sie bitte, Herr Denery. Die gnaedige Frau wunscht dass Sie nach oben kommen. Sie hatt ein kleines Geschaenck aus New Orleans fur Sie mitgebracht.]
NICK. (*In German.*) [No. Tell Mrs. Denery I will see her in the

31

morning. Tell her to take a sleeping pill.] [Sagen Sie der gnaedigen Frau ich werde sie Morgen sehn. Sagen Sie Ihr sie soll ein Schlafmittel nehmen.]

HILDA. (*In German.*) [Thank you, sir.] *Danke, Mein Herr.*

CONSTANCE. (*Who hasn't understood the German but who is puzzled because* SOPHIE *is frowning and* GRIGGS *has turned away.*) Can I—does Nina want something? (SOPHIE *picks up sheet, puts it on bed.*)

NICK. No, no. She's fine. (SOPHIE *begins to make up couch.* NICK *turns to her. Very gracious.*) That means one of us must have put you out of your room. I'm sorry and I thank you.

SOPHIE. Not at all, sir. It is nothing.

NICK. (*Comes to her.*) You're a sweet child and I look forward to knowing you. Good night.

SOPHIE. Good night.

NICK. (*To* GRIGGS.) Good night, sir. A great pleasure. (CONSTANCE *crosses* U. *to hall door.* GRIGGS *bows.* NICK *crosses, kisses* CONSTANCE *on cheek.*) Wonderful to be here, darling. (*He goes out.* CONSTANCE *looks after him, then moves to help* SOPHIE *make up couch.* SOPHIE *hands her two sofa pillows. She puts them on phone chair. Silence for a minute while they arrange bedclothes.* GRIGGS *crosses* R. *above to above table.*)

CONSTANCE. (*At* R. *of sofa. Lightly.*) What did the German maid want? Something from the kitchen? I suppose I shouldn't ask, but what did she want? (*No answer.*) Sophie. (SOPHIE *looks up, then* D. *and back to work. No answer.*) Sophie.

SOPHIE. (*Slowly.*) Mrs. Denery wanted to say good night to Mr. Denery. (*Crosses, gets sheet from chair, crosses back to* L. *of sofa.*)

GRIGGS. (*Sits* R. *of table.*) Mrs. Denery had bought a little gift for him in New Orleans and wanted to give it to him. (*Looks at book.*)

CONSTANCE. After all these years. To have a little gift for him. Isn't that nice? (GRIGGS *looks at her. She looks at* GRIGGS *and* SOPHIE. GRIGGS *looks away. Neither answers her. She becomes conscious of something strained.*) What did Nick say?

SOPHIE. (*Above* L. *end of sofa, tucking in blanket.*) He said she should take a sleeping pill and go to sleep.

CONSTANCE. Why, Sophie. Are you disturbed about something, dear? (*Crosses to her above sofa. Looks at her dress.*) You didn't

32

go to the party! I've been so busy, I didn't realize —— Why, where's Fred and ——?

SOPHIE. I did not wish to go to the party, Aunt Constance. And Frederick had a most important appointment.

CONSTANCE. More important than being with you? Young people get engaged and act toward each other with such—I don't know. (*To* GRIGGS. *Crosses to* R. *end of sofa, tucks sheet in.*) In our day we made marriage more romantic and I must say I think we had more fun. If you can't have fine dreams now, then when can you have them? (SOPHIE *looks at her. Crosses above sofa, pats* SOPHIE. *Sighing.*) Never mind. I guess the new way is more sensible. But I liked our way better. (*To* GRIGGS, *who looks up.*) Didn't you? (*Crosses* R. *to* L. *of table.* SOPHIE *crosses, gets pillow and blanket from chair, puts them on bed.*) Oh, what's the matter with me? I forgot; Rose came back from the party. She said she was ill: I mean, I think she just didn't feel well —— Carrie is upstairs with her. (*He doesn't move.*) I think Carrie probably wants to go back to the party and is waiting for you to come.

GRIGGS. Yes. Of course. Thank you. Good night.

CONSTANCE. Good night.

GRIGGS. Good night, Sophie.

SOPHIE. Good night, General. (*He exits upstairs.*)

CONSTANCE. (*Crossing to above sofa to* SOPHIE. *She kisses* SOPHIE *on cheek.*) You'll be comfortable? See you in the morning, dear. (*Crosses to table, gets portrait, looks at* SOPHIE, *then she exits through hall.* SOPHIE *crosses* D. *to chair* L. *of sofa, gets pajamas and robe, crosses to above sofa, puts them on it. She then starts to unzip dress, as* CROSSMAN *enters from stairs in shirt-sleeves.*)

CROSSMAN. (*Crossing* L. *to bookcase, gets book.*) Excuse me. I need another book and another bottle, Sophie. (*Crosses* L. *to upstage table on porch, gets brandy bottle.*) I tell you these two weeks of respectability each summer are getting me down. When I was eight months old I knew I'd have to break with it. Royal Denery's gone to bed? Does anybody improve with age? Just tell me that and I'll have something to lie awake and think about. (*Crosses* R. *toward hall door.*)

SOPHIE. I do not know, Mr. Ned.

CROSSMAN. (*Turns back at* U. C.) For God's sake, Sophie, have an opinion about something! Try it and see what comes out!

33

SOPHIE. (*Sits upstage* R. *side of sofa, facing upstage.*) Some people improve with age, some do not.

CROSSMAN. (*Crossing to* U. R. *of sofa.*) Wonderful, Sophie, wonderful. Some people improve with age, some do not. As profound as it is silly. Who do you think you're fooling, kid? You never were a brilliant girl, but at least when you came here you were normal. You keep on with that pseudo-stupidity and in another five years you won't be *pseudo*-stupid.

SOPHIE. I will not mind. It will be easier. Please do not feel sorry or notice me so much, Mr. Ned.

CROSSMAN. (*Crossing down stage at chair* L. *of table.*) You came here a nice little girl who had seen war and trouble. You had spirit in a quiet way, and you were gay, in a quiet way, which is the only way women should be gay, since they are never really gay at all. Only serious people are ever gay. And women are very seldom serious people. They are earnest instead, but earnestness hasn't anything to do with seriousness. . . . What the hell is this marriage business between you and Fred Ellis?

SOPHIE. (*Rises, crossing* L. *to behind chair* L. *of sofa.*) It is the marriage business between me and Fred Ellis.

CROSSMAN. But what's the matter with you? Haven't you got sense enough to know ——?

SOPHIE. I do the best I can. I do the best I can. And I thank you for worrying about me . . .

CROSSMAN. (*Sitting* R. *end of sofa.*) Sure I worry about you. Given this much to drink I worry about a great many things, and I am convinced that it has been given to me to understand that which I may not understand again. A little later in the evening, I don't worry about much, and am not so certain that I see the truth, or I get bored . . . Right now I've had just enough (*Rises.*) . . . Look here: I was born into this world, went through it, and came out below it. It hasn't got much, unless you want it easy . . . and this kind of "easy" *isn't* easy. What do *you* want with it? (*Crosses* R. *to below* R. *end of sofa.*) Turn yourself around, girl, and go back where you belong. Beat it, quick.

SOPHIE. (*Almost pitying him.*) You take many words to say simple things. All of you. Go home, shall I? Just like that, you say it. Aunt Constance has used up all her money on me, wasted it, and for why and what? How can I go home?

CROSSMAN. If that's all it is I'll find you the money to go home.

SOPHIE. (*Wearily.*) Oh, Mr. Ned. We owe money in our village, my mother and I. In my kind of Europe you can't live where you owe money. Go home! (*Helplessly.*) Did I ever want to come? I have no place here and I am lost and homesick. I *like* my mother, I —— Every night I plan to go. But it is five years now and there is no plan and no chance to find one. Therefore . . . I will do the best I can. (*Very sharply, to avoid crying.*) And I will not cry about it and I will not speak of it again.

CROSSMAN. (*Softly, as if he were moved.*) The best you can?

SOPHIE. I think so. (*Sweetly.*) Maybe you've never tried to do that, Mr. Ned. Maybe none of you have tried.

CROSSMAN. (*Crossing* R. *above sofa to* U. R. *of sofa.*) Yes, Sophie, lonely people talking to each other can make each other lonelier. They should be careful, because maybe lonely people are the only people who can't afford to cry. I'm sorry. (*Crosses* U., *turns in door.*) I'm sorry. (*He looks at her, smiles, amused. She smiles at him. He exits through hall, closes sliding door as curtain falls.*)

## CURTAIN

# ACT II

## Scene 1

SCENE: *Same as ACT I. A week later, eight-thirty, Sunday morning.*

AT RISE: CONSTANCE *is standing against living-room pillar of porch.* NICK *is standing in front of an easel.* CONSTANCE *has on a most unbecoming house dress and her hair is drawn back tight. She looks ten years older. In living-room* SOPHIE *has finished folding her bedclothes and is hurrying around the room with a carpet sweeper. After a second* LEON *appears from upstage of porch and moves out to porch. He puts upstage table down stage.* CONSTANCE *tries desperately to ask him if everything is all right in the kitchen. She does this by moving her lips and trying not to move her head.* LEON *sees her motions but doesn't understand what she is trying to say. The noise of this and the carpet sweeper becomes sharp.* SOPHIE, *below table working carpet sweeper, moves* L. *to above sofa.* LEON *puts large upstage table* R. *of easel, ducking between* CONSTANCE *and* NICK.

NICK. (*Irritated.*) Constance, please ask them to stop that noise. (*Waves hand to* LEON *and* SOPHIE.) Go away, both of you.

CONSTANCE. They can't, Nick. I explain it to you every morning! We simply have to get ready for breakfast. (*Turns upstage. Quietly.*) Sophie, is everything all right in the kitchen?

SOPHIE. (*At above sofa.*) Yes, ma'am. Everything is fine. (*Leaves sweeper above sofa, crosses* D., *gets bedclothes, exits into hall.*)

NICK. (*To* CONSTANCE, *sharply.*) Please keep the pose. (*Quieter.*) Just a few minutes more. (*LEON starts* U.)

CONSTANCE. (*Turning to* LEON, *who crosses* D. *to her* L.) Leon, tell Sadie not to cook the liver until everybody is downstairs, like she always does. Did she remember about the grits this Sunday? (*To* NICK, *sees his face.*) All right, I'm sorry. But really, I can't run a guest house, and pose for —— (*She sighs, settles back.*

36

LEON *finishes with porch table and comes back into living room as* MRS. ELLIS *comes down steps.*)

MRS. ELLIS. (*At* U. C. *To* LEON.) My breakfast ready?

LEON. (*Takes carpet sweeper above sofa.*) No, ma'am. We'll ring the bell.

MRS. ELLIS. What's the matter with my breakfast?

LEON. Nothing the matter with it. It will be like always.

MRS. ELLIS. It gets later and later every day.

LEON. No, ma'am. That's just you. Want it in the dining room or on the porch?

MRS. ELLIS. (*Crossing* L. *to* U. L. *of sofa. Enjoying it.*) Too damp on the porch. Whole house is damp. I haven't slept all summer, Leon.

LEON. Just as well not to sleep in summer.

MRS. ELLIS. You're going to have to explain that to me some time. (LEON *exits into hall. She turns, goes toward porch, comes to* U. L. *of easel.*) Constance, he's made you look right mean and ten years older. Why have you done that, Nicholas?

NICK. (*To* MRS. ELLIS.) Shoo, shoo. This is forbidden ground.

MRS. ELLIS. (*Crossing* U. *to* L. *of* CONSTANCE. *To* CONSTANCE.) Ten years older! When you pay an artist to paint your portrait he makes you ten years younger. I had my portrait done when I was twenty-one, holding my first baby. And the baby looked older than I did. Was rather a scandal or like those people in Tennessee.

NICK. (*Crossing* U. *to her. Kidding, but slightly annoyed.*) You know if you wouldn't interrupt me every morning, I think I'd fall in love with you. (SOPHIE *enters from hall with coffee urn, cups, sugar and cream on table tray, puts it* U. R.)

MRS. ELLIS. I wouldn't like that. Even if I was the right age I wouldn't like it. Although I realize it would make me dangerously different from every other woman in the world. (*Crosses* R. *into living-room.*) You would never have been my dish of tea, and isn't that a silly way of saying it? Sophie, give me a cup, I have to stay awake for church. (SOPHIE *crosses* L. *to* C. *with coffee and sugar, gives coffee to* MRS. ELLIS, *puts 3 lumps of sugar in it. To* SOPHIE.) You're the only one who ever remembers about my sugar. (*Crosses* R. *above table to* R. *of table, sits.* CROSSMAN *comes down steps and into the room. Crossing* U. R., *gets cup of coffee.* CROSSMAN *crosses to* U. R. *of sofa.*) Good morning, Ned.

CROSSMAN. Good morning.

37

MRS. ELLIS. (*Crossing* R. *to* R. *of table.* SOPHIE *crosses to above table.*) Tell me, what shall I give Sophie for her wedding present? My pearls, or my mother's diamonds?

CROSSMAN. (*To* SOPHIE.) The rich always give something old and precious to their new brides. Something that doesn't cost them *new money.* Same thing true in your country?

SOPHIE. I do not know the rich in my country. (*Crosses* U. R., *puts sugar down, gets two cups of coffee.*)

MRS. ELLIS. He's quite right, Sophie. Not only something old but something so old that we're sick of it.

CROSSMAN. (*Dryly.*) Why don't you give her a nice new check?

MRS. ELLIS. Only if I have to. (SOPHIE *starts for porch with coffee.*)

CONSTANCE. (*Can't go on any more. On porch.*) Nick, my neck is breaking ——

NICK. (*Slightly annoyed.*) All right. All finished for this morning. (*Puts brushes, paint-box against down stage porch pillar. Turns picture around so that* CONSTANCE *cannot see it.* SOPHIE *brings two cups of coffee to porch, to above table.*)

CONSTANCE. (*Collapsing in a chair* R. *of table.*) Whew! (*Takes coffee from* SOPHIE, *pats her arm.* SOPHIE *takes other cup to* NICK. CROSSMAN *crosses* L. *on to porch to* L. *side opposite doors.*)

NICK. (*At* L. *of table.*) You're the girl I want to paint. Change your mind and we'll start today. Why not, Sophie?

SOPHIE. I am not pretty, Mr. Nicholas.

NICK. You are better than pretty. (*Puts coffee* D. *on table. Puts portrait on paint-box against pillar, puts easel* D. L. SOPHIE *moves off upstage exit of porch.*)

CROSSMAN. (*Crossing* D. *few steps. Staring at* CONSTANCE.) My God, you look awful, Constance! What did you get done up like that for? You're poor enough not to have to pretend you are poor. (NINA *enters.*)

NICK. (*Pulls chair from* D. L. *to* L. *of table. Laughing.*) Go way, Ned. You've got a hangover. I know I have. (NINA *comes down steps, comes into room, says good morning to* MRS. ELLIS, *who says good morning to her. She crosses to* U. R., *pours herself cup of coffee.*)

CONSTANCE. (*Curiously.*) You know, I waited up until twelve o'clock for you both ——

NICK. We were late. We had a good get-together last night. Like

38

old times, wasn't it, Ned? (NINA *crosses* L. *to porch door, hears conversation. To* CONSTANCE.) If you have the normal vanity you'd be pleased at the amount of time we spent on you. Ned loosened up and talked ——

CROSSMAN. (*Sharply.*) I did? I thought that was you.

NICK. (*Laughs.*) I knew you wouldn't remember what you'd said —— Don't regret it: did you good to speak your heart out—for once.

CROSSMAN. My heart, eh? (*Turns upstage few steps.*)

NICK. (*To* CONSTANCE. *Slyly.*) In a juke-box song called "Constance."

CONSTANCE. What? I don't understand. (NINA *crosses* R. *slowly to above sofa.*)

CROSSMAN. (*Crossing* D. *to above table. Has turned sharply, then decided to laugh.*) Neither do I. The stage of not remembering, or speaking out my heart, will come in time, I am sorry to say. But I hope it hasn't come yet. (*Crosses into living-room to* NINA.)

NINA. (*A little timidly.*) Good morning, Mr. Crossman.

CROSSMAN. Good morning, Mrs. Denery. I'm sorry you didn't join us last night—to hear me pour my heart out.

NINA. I'm never invited to the pouring of a heart.

CROSSMAN. I looked for you, but Nick said you had a headache.

NINA. (*Lightly.*) Nick always says I have a headache when he doesn't want me to come along, or sees to it that I do have one. (LEON *enters in hall, rings bell.* NINA *crosses* R. *to* R. *of sofa, sits.*)

MRS. ELLIS. (*Gets up quickly, crosses* U., *puts cup on tray* U. R.) All right, Leon. I'm ready. I haven't eaten since four this morning. (LEON *exits.* MRS. ELLIS *goes out. As she passes stairs, she shouts up.*) Carrie! Frederick! I simply won't wait breakfast any longer. (CROSSMAN *puts cup on phone table, follows her out.* CONSTANCE *rises, crosses* U. *to* L. *of porch door.*)

CONSTANCE. (*At door.*) Well, they seemed to have managed in the kitchen without me. I reckon I better change now. (*Crosses* D. *few steps.*) Where did you get this dress, Nick! (*Crosses* D. *to above table.*)

NICK. Place on Dreyenen Street.

CONSTANCE. (*Appalled that it is so cheap.*) In a Negro store! You bought this dress in a Negro store! (*He looks at her and laughs.*) I don't mean that. I mean Ned's right. You must have wanted to make me look just about as awful as —— (NINA *rises,*

39

crosses L. *to upstage side of porch door.*) For some reason I don't understand. Nick, what *are* you doing? (*Suspiciously.*) And why won't you let me see the portrait?

NICK. (*Sincerely.*) Haven't you yet figured out that Ned is jealous?

CONSTANCE. Jealous of what? (NINA *crosses* D., *sits* L. *arm of sofa.*)

NICK. He's in love with you, girl. As much as he was when we were kids. You're all he talked about last night. How lonely he's been, how much he's wanted you, how often he asked you to marry him ——

CONSTANCE. (*Incredulously.*) I just don't believe you. Ned never talks about himself. I just don't believe he said such things ——

NICK. You know damn well he loves you and you know he's rotting away for you. He said last night ——

CONSTANCE. (*Prissy.*) Nick, if he did talk and it's *most* out of character, I don't think I should hear what he said in confidence just to you.

NICK. Oh, run along, honey. You're as pleased as punch. (NICK *smiles, she smiles and exits upstage on porch.* NICK *puts coffee on table upstage as* NINA *comes out to porch, crossing* U. *to her above table.*) Morning, darling. What's the matter?

NINA. Why have you done that? To Constance?

NICK. Done what? Tell her the truth? (*They kiss.*)

NINA. How could you know it to be the truth? (NICK *crosses* L. *to chair* L. *of table.*) I don't believe Crossman talked to you —— (*Sits chair* R. *of table.* NICK *folds easel, puts it against porch pillar.* LEON *enters, puts tray on table, pours coffee, takes cup from* NINA, *crosses* U., *then puts pot on little table upstage, picks up coffee cups, exits upstage.*)

NICK. Look, it makes her happy—and if I can get a little sense into her head it will make *him* happy. I don't have to have an affidavit to know what's going on in the human heart. (*Sits down* L. *of table, starts to eat breakfast.*)

NINA. (*Laughs.*) Oh, you are enjoying yourself so much here. (*Leans back in chair.*) I've seldom seen it this hog-wild. You're on a rampage of good-will. Makes me nervous for even the trees outside.

NICK. (*Laughs.*) I don't know what you're talking about. (*They eat in silence for a moment.*)

40

NINA. (*Serious now.*) Are *we* staying much longer, Nick?

NICK. A few more days. The house officially closes this week, Constance says. The Ellises go tomorrow and the Griggs on Tuesday. I think. Just till I finish. (ROSE *comes down stairs, carrying small overnight case. She is done up in a pretty, too fussy hat and a pretty, too fussy dress. She looks in room, puts case down, R. of phone table, comes hurrying to porch door.*)

NINA. Finish what?

NICK. (*Carefully.*) The portrait, Nina.

ROSE. (*At below bookcase.*) Oh, good morning. Sorry to interrupt. You look so handsome together. (*Makes gesture to* NICK *meaning "Could you come here?"*) Nick ——

NICK. (*Hospitable.*) Come on out.

ROSE. I'd rather. Could you ——

NICK. Come and join us.

ROSE. (*Crossing* D. *to above table. Hesitantly.*) Well, I wanted to tell *you* but I don't want to worry Nina —— (*Looking at* NINA.) You see ——

NINA. I'd go away, Mrs. Griggs, but I've been dismissed from so many meals lately that I'm getting hungry.

ROSE. (*Smiles to* NINA. *Speaks to* NICK.) I called him last night. Just like you advised. And I'm driving right over now. He's the executor of my trust fund, you know. He's very wise: (*To* NINA.) I've got gilt-edged securities.

NICK. Who is *this?*

ROSE. My brother, of course. Henry, like I told you. (*To* NINA.) It sounds so mysterious, but it isn't. He's much older. You know he builds ships, I mean during our wars. I'll tell him the whole story, Nick, and he'll know what to do.

NICK. (*Sits* L. *of table, expecting her to leave, starts to eat. Amused.*) Of course he will.

ROSE. I'm going to drive over to my doctor's. He's going to wait for me on a hot Sunday. It'll be expensive —— (*To* NINA, *boasting slightly.*) I had a heart murmur. They had to take me out of school for a year.

NINA. Recently? (NICK *chokes back a laugh, then* ROSE *gets it.*)

ROSE. (*Giggles.*) That's charming—"recently"! (*To* NICK.) There's so much I wanted to consult you about. I waited up for you last night, but—well. Should I do just as you told me yesterday?

NICK. (*Who doesn't remember what he told her.*) Sure.

41

ROSE. Everything?

NICK. Well ——

NINA. (*With a lift.*) I think, Mrs. Griggs, you'll have to remind Nick what he told you. Yesterday is a long time ago when you have so many ladies to attend to ——

ROSE. (*Back upstage as* NICK *laughs, partly from embarrassment.*) I shouldn't have brought it up like this. (*Crosses back* D.) Oh, Mrs. Denery, you might as well know: it's about a divorce, and Nick has been most kind.

NINA. (*Rises, crossing* R. *around chair to down stage door pillar.*) I am sure of it.

ROSE. (*Crossing, sits* R. *of table.*) Just one more thing. What should I do about our boys? Should I telephone them, or let Henry? One of our sons works on the atom bomb, you know. He's the religious one. What do you think, Nick?

NINA. (*Trying not to laugh, moves away.*) Goodness! (*Crosses* L. *to edge of porch.*)

NICK. (*Takes her hand, rises, she rises and they move into living-room to above sofa. Covering.*) I think you should go and have your breakfast. It's my firm belief that women only look well in hats after they've eaten.

ROSE. (*To* NICK, *softly, secretly happily.*) And I'm going to just make Henry commission the portrait —— (NINA *crosses* R. *above table, sits* R. *of table.*) You remember though that I told you my niece can't take the braces off her teeth for another six months.

NICK. (*Laughs.*) Go along now, my dear. (*Crosses back, sits* L. *of table.*)

ROSE. (*Pleased. Grateful.*) Thank you for all you've done. And forgive me, Nina. (*She exits upstage.*)

NICK. (*Looks up at her.*) There was a day when we would have laughed together about that. Don't you have fun any more?

NINA. I don't think so.

NICK. She's quite nice, really. And very funny.

NINA. (*Partly amused, partly irritated.*) I suppose it's all right to flirt with, or to charm, women and men and children and animals, but nowadays it seems to me you include red squirrels, sirloin steaks, lamp shades and books-in-vellum. (SOPHIE *enters from hall with tray and vase of flowers, puts them on cabinet* U. R.)

NICK. (*Smiles.*) Are you crazy? (CARRIE *enters and speaks.*) Flirt with that silly woman? Eat your breakfast, Nina. I've had

42

enough seriousness where none is due. (*Lights cigarette. Through this speech* CARRIE *has come down steps. She sees* SOPHIE, *who is* U. R.)

CARRIE. (*Crossing to below hall door.*) Good morning, dear. Is Frederick in the dining-room?

SOPHIE. (*At* U. R.) No. He has not come down as yet. (*Crosses* D. R., *opens doors.* CARRIE *continues on to porch.*)

CARRIE. (*Crossing to above table. To* NICK *and* NINA.) Good morning. Your maid said you wanted to see me, Nick. (SOPHIE *crosses, gets cup from phone table, crosses back* R., *puts it on butler's tray. Then arranges flowers in vase.*)

NICK. (*Rises, gets chair from upstage, puts it above table. Hesitantly, because of* NINA'S *presence.*) Carrie, I hesitated all day yesterday. I told myself perhaps you knew, but maybe, just maybe, you didn't.

NINA. (*Laughs.*) Oh, it sounds so serious.

CARRIE. (*Smiles.*) It does indeed. (*Sits above table.*)

NICK. (*Looks at* NINA. *Carefully.*) Don't you know that man's reputation, Carrie? You can't travel around Europe with him. (*Sits* L. *of table.*)

CARRIE. Travel around Europe with *him?* I'm going to Europe with Frederick. (*Then sharply, as she sees his face.*) What do you mean, Nick?

NICK. I ——

CARRIE. Please tell me.

NICK. (*Confidentially.*) I saw Frederick in the travel agency yesterday with a man I once met in Europe. Not the sort of man you'd expect to see Frederick with.

CARRIE. Are you talking about Mr. Payson?

NICK. Yes, I am. Well, I waited until they left the travel place and then I went in. (SOPHIE *crosses with tray to porch, puts orange juice glasses on tray, crosses* U., *gets coffee pot.*)

NINA. (*Suspiciously.*) Why did you go in?

NICK. (*To* NINA.) Luther hadn't seen me since we were kids, and we got to talking. (*To* CARRIE.) He said he had booked your passage on the Elizabeth and now he had another for Mr. Payson and Fred had just paid for it —— (CARRIE *gets up, turns sharply, does not speak.*) I didn't know whether you knew, Carrie, or if I should tell you —— (SOPHIE *exits upstage with dishes and coffee pot.*)

CARRIE. (*Turns back.*) I didn't know. I thank you for telling me. (*At above table. After a second, she turns.*) What did you mean, Nick, when you asked me if I knew Payson's reputation? I don't like to press you for gossip, but ——

NINA. He didn't mean anything, Mrs. Ellis ——

NICK. Oh, look here, Nina, you know he's part of the Count Dinos set, and on the nasty fringe of that.

CARRIE. (*Annoyed.*) What does that mean: the Count Dinos' set and the nasty fringe of that?

NINA. (*Trying to stop it. Quickly.*) It means very little. The Count is a foolish old man who gives large parties ——

NICK. (*To* NINA.) Would you want your young son with such people at such parties?

NINA. (*Angrily. Rises.*) I have no son. And I don't know: perhaps I would have wanted only to leave him alone —— (*Crosses* R. *to behind* R. *chair.*)

CARRIE. (*Gently.*) All people who have no children think that, Mrs. Denery. But it just isn't true. (*Sits above table. To* NICK.) I don't know much about Mr. Payson, but I've been worried for a long time that he's taken Frederick in. Frederick admires his writing, and —— Yet I know so little about him. He stayed with us a few weeks in town last winter. He'd just come back from Europe then ——

NICK. He'd just come back from a filthy little scandal in Rome. It was all over the papers.

NINA. You don't know it was true.

CARRIE. What kind of scandal? (*No answer, softly.*) Please help me. I don't understand.

NICK. (*Slightly impatient.*) Look, Carrie, there's nothing to understand. The guy is just no good. That's all you need to know. He's nobody to travel around Europe with.

CARRIE. How could Fred have ——? (*She hesitates a moment, rises.*) It was kind and friendly of you to tell me. (*Indicating she has a plan of action.*) I am grateful to you both. (*She goes slowly upstage, exits.* NINA *crosses* U. *angrily, turns on him. Long pause:* NICK *takes sip of coffee, looks around at* NINA.)

NICK. What would you have done?

NINA. (*Sits above table. Idly.*) I don't know. Have you ever tried leaving things alone?

NICK. I like Carrie. She doesn't know what the hell it's all about—

and the chances are the boy doesn't either. I'm sorry for them. Aren't you? (*When she doesn't answer.*) What's the matter, Nina?

NINA. (*Here we go again.*) I can smell it: it's all around us. The flower-like odor right before it becomes troublesome and heavy. It travels ahead of you, Nick, whenever you get most helpful, most loving and most lovable. Down through the years it runs ahead of us—I smell it—and I want to leave.

NICK. (*Puts out cigarette. Rises, pushes his chair to table, stands behind it. Pleasantly.*) I think maybe you're one of the few neurotics in the world who didn't marry a neurotic. I wonder how that happened?

NINA. *I want to leave.*

NICK. (*Coldly.*) Then leave.

NINA. (*Rises, to* R. *of chair above table. After a second, slightly tremulous.*) You won't come?

NICK. (*Quietly—firmly.*) I told you: we'll go Friday. If you want to go before, then go. But stop talking about it, Nina. (*Gently.*) Or we'll be in for one of your long farewells—and long returns. I don't think I can stand another. (*Comes to her, puts hands on her shoulders.*) Spare yourself, darling. You pay so heavy, inside. Friday, then. And in the meantime, gentle down to the pretty lady you truly are. (*He kisses her. Exits* L. NINA *stands quietly for a moment.* SOPHIE *comes on to porch from upstage.*)

SOPHIE. (*Crossing* D. *to* L. *of* NINA. *Gently, sensing something has happened.*) Would you like something, Mrs. Denery?

NINA. (*Softly.*) No, thank you. (SOPHIE *straightens chairs.* NINA *moves off, through the room and toward staircase. As she crosses below phone table,* FREDERICK *comes in.*)

FREDERICK. Good morning.

NINA. Good morning, Mr. Ellis. (*Stops as if she wanted to tell him something.*) I'd like —— Good morning. (*She goes up as* SOPHIE, *who has heard their voices, leaves dishes and comes quickly into room.*)

SOPHIE. (*Crossing into living-room,* U. L. *of sofa. Calling into hall.*) Fred. Fred. Would you like to have your breakfast on the kitchen porch? (*Points upstage.*)

FREDERICK. (*Crossing* L. *a step.*) Sure. Why?

SOPHIE. Your mother is—er —— (*Crosses* R. *to him. Points toward dining-room.*) She has found out that —— Come.

FREDERICK. Denery told her he saw me in the travel agency. I was

45

sure he would. There's nothing to worry about. I intended to tell her this morning.

SOPHIE. But perhaps it would be more wise to wait.

FREDERICK. (*Smiles to her.*) We'll be leaving here tomorrow, and for Europe on the sixteenth. (*Takes her D. to sofa.*) You and I won't see each other for six months. Sophie, you're sure you feel all right about my going? (*Seats her on C. of sofa. Sits on her R.*)

SOPHIE. (*Quickly.*) Oh, I do. We did not arrange any date of time for the wedding.

FREDERICK. (*Being helpful to her. Smiles.*) I don't think you want a date of time, Sophie. And you don't have to be ashamed of wishing you could find another way. But if there isn't any other way for you, then I'll be just as good to you as I know how. And I know you will be to me.

SOPHIE. You are a kind man. And I will also be kind, I hope.

FREDERICK. It isn't any deal for you.

SOPHIE. (*Puts hand up to her mouth. Cheerfully.*) It will be nice in your house with you, and I will be grateful for it.

FREDERICK. I *have* no house, Sophie. People like me never have their own house, so to speak.

SOPHIE. (*Reassuring him.*) Never mind. Whatever house. It will be nice. We will make it so. (*He smiles, pats her arm.*)

FREDERICK. Mother in the dining room? (*Rises, crossing U. to hall. She nods.*) Might as well face it out. (*Stops at hall door as she speaks.*)

SOPHIE. (*Rises, crosses U. around R. of sofa to hall door, calling to him.*) I would not. No, I would not. (FRED *exits into hall.*) All of you face out too much. Every act of life should not be of such importance —— (*Crosses toward porch, talking to herself. Exits upstage of porch.* FREDERICK *comes back into room, crosses D. to above table. After a moment,* CARRIE *appears from hall, cigarette in hand. She comes into room, crosses D. to R. of sofa, obviously very disturbed. But she does not speak.*)

FREDERICK. There's nothing to be so upset about.

CARRIE. (*After a pause.*) You think that, really? (*Crosses L. to coffee table, puts cigarette out in ash-tray.* MRS. ELLIS *appears in hall. She leaves hat on hall table, carries black bag and gloves into room.*)

FREDERICK. We're going to have a companion. That's all. We know nothing of traveling and Payson knows all of Europe.

46

MRS. ELLIS. (*Crossing* D. *to* U. C.) Of course. You're lucky to get Mr. Payson to come along. (CARRIE *crosses* D. L. *of living-room. Both turn to look at her.*)

FREDERICK. (*After a second, to* CARRIE.) What is it, Mother? (*A pause because of* MRS. ELLIS' *presence.*)

CARRIE. (*Crossing* U. *to behind chair* L. *of sofa.*) It's shocking of you to take along a guest without consulting me. You and I have planned this trip for three years and ——

FREDERICK. I didn't consult you because the idea came up quickly and Payson had to get his ticket before the travel office closed for the week-end ——

CARRIE. (*Crossing to* L. *of sofa.*) Payson had to get *his* ticket?

FREDERICK. I thought you'd given up going through my checkbooks?

CARRIE. Please don't speak that way to me. (*Pause, quietly, delicately.*) We are not going to Europe.

FREDERICK. (*After a second, quietly but definitely.*) I am.

CARRIE. We are not going, Fred. We are not going.

MRS. ELLIS. (*Crossing* D. *to him.*) Your mother's feelings are hurt. She had looked forward to being alone with you. Of course.

FREDERICK. (*Uncomfortably.*) We'll still be together.

CARRIE. (*Crossing* R. *to above* C. *of sofa. To* MRS. ELLIS, *sharply.*) I don't wish to be interpreted, Mother. (MRS. ELLIS *crosses* R. *to above chair* R., R. *of* FREDERICK. *To* FREDERICK, *as to a child.*) There's no sense talking about it: we'll go another time.

FREDERICK. (*Crossing to her.*) Will you stop acting as if you're taking me back to school? (CARRIE *crosses* L. *to* U. L. *of sofa.* FREDERICK *follows.*) I will be disappointed if you don't wish to come with me, but I am sailing on the sixteenth. (CARRIE *turns back.* FREDERICK *crosses* R. *few steps. Then, rather desperately.*) I've never had much fun. Never seen the things I wished to see, never met the people I wanted to meet, or been the places where I could. There are wonderful things to see and to learn about and to try to understand. We're lucky to have somebody who knows about them and who is willing to have *us* tag along. *I'm* not much to drag around —— (*Crosses* L. *above sofa to* CARRIE. *Giving in, softly.*) I'll come back, and you can take up my life again. Six months isn't much to ask.

MRS. ELLIS. (*Crossing* L. *to above chair* L. *of table. Not sad.*) Six months? Sad to ask so little.

47

CARRIE. (*As if she recognized a tone of voice.*) Mother, please. I ——

MRS. ELLIS. (*Goading him on.*) Perhaps you won't want to come back at all? I wouldn't blame you. (*Puts bag and gloves on table.*)

CARRIE. (*Nervously.*) Fred, don't make a decision now. Promise me you'll think about it until tomorrow, and then we'll talk quietly and ——

MRS. ELLIS. (*Crossing* U. *a step.* To FREDERICK.) Don't make bargains with your mother. Everything always ends that way between you. I advise you to go now, or stay.

FREDERICK. (*Firmly, to* MRS. ELLIS.) I am going. (*To* CARRIE.) There is nothing to think about. I'm going. (*He turns and exits up staircase. There is a pause.* MRS. ELLIS *crosses* R. *to above chair* R. *of table.*)

CARRIE. (*Crossing* R. *to* C. *Quietly. Angry.*) You always do that, Mother. You always arrange to come out his friend and make me his enemy. You've been amusing yourself that way all his life.

MRS. ELLIS. There's no time for all that, Carrie. I warned you to say and do nothing. I told you to make the best of it and go along with them.

CARRIE. (*Softly.*) How could I do that? Payson is a scoundrel and Fred doesn't know it, and won't believe it. (*Crosses* L. *to* R. *of sofa.*) What am I to do now?

MRS. ELLIS. (*Crossing* L. *to above chair* L. *of table. An order.*) You're to go upstairs and say that you are reconciled to his leaving without you, but that Frederick is to make clear to his guest that his ten thousand a year ends today and will not begin again.

CARRIE. (*Sits* R. *end of sofa. Sharply. Pleading.*) I couldn't do that. He'd hate me for it. Maybe we'd better let him go, and perhaps I can join him later. Time will —— (*Rises. Defeated. Sees* MRS. ELLIS' *face.*) I will not cut off his allowance.

MRS. ELLIS. (*Turns back* L. *Sharply.*) I didn't know it was you who wrote the check. (CARRIE *winces slightly.*)

CARRIE. (*With dignity.*) Are you quite sure you wish to speak this way?

MRS. ELLIS. (*At above chair* L. *of table.*) Relatively sure.

CARRIE. Then I will say as sharply that the money is his father's money, and not yours to threaten him, or deprive him, in any proper sense.

MRS. ELLIS. (*Slightly angry.*) In any *proper* sense. There is no

48

morality to money, Carrie, and very immoral of you to think so.
CARRIE. (*A threat.*) If you stop his allowance, Mother, I will simply send him mine.
MRS. ELLIS. Then I will not give you yours. (*Crosses to* U. R. *sofa.* MRS. ELLIS *now speaks gently. This is her philosophy.*) Yes, old people are often harsh, Carrie, when they control the purse. You'll see, when your day comes. And then, too, one comes to be bored with those who fool themselves. I say to myself—one should have power, or give it over. But if one keeps it, it might as well be used, with as little mealy-mouthness as possible. Go up now, and press him hard, and do it straight. (*Dismissing her. Contemptuous.*) Tell yourself you're doing it for his own good. (*Crosses* R. *to above table, gets bag and gloves.*)
CARRIE. (*At* U. R. *of sofa. Softly.*) I wouldn't be doing it otherwise.
MRS. ELLIS. (*Putting on gloves.*) Perhaps. Perhaps not. Doesn't really matter. (*Laughs, amused.* CARRIE *crosses* U., *slowly to hall.*) I'm off to church now. You can skip church today, Carrie.
CARRIE. Thank you for the dispensation.
MRS. ELLIS. (*To* CARRIE, *as* CARRIE *moves off upstairs.*) Quite all right. You have God's work to do. (*Crosses* U., *gets hat from hall table, puts it on.* ROSE *enters, crosses* D. R., *looks out door, crosses* L., *sits* C. *of sofa.* MRS. ELLIS *turns to watch* ROSE, *who is elaborately settling herself on sofa as if she were arranging for a scene —which is what she is doing.* MRS. ELLIS, *in hall.*) What are you doing, Mrs. Griggs? (ROSE *nervously points to* R. *window.* MRS. ELLIS *looks toward it, watches* ROSE *fix her face.*) Is it Robert Taylor you're expecting, or Vice-President Barkley? (GRIGGS *comes in from the* R. *windows.*) Oh.
GRIGGS. (*In* D. R. *door. To them both.*) Good morning.
MRS. ELLIS. Your wife's getting ready to flirt. You'd be safer in church with me. (*She exits* U. R. *as* GRIGGS *laughs. He goes toward coffee urn* U. R., *pours cup of coffee.*)
ROSE. (*Meaning* MRS. ELLIS.) Nasty old thing. (*Then, putting on gloves.*) I'm driving over to see him. I'm sorry I had to make such a decision, but I felt it was necessary now.
GRIGGS. Are you talking about your brother? (*Sips coffee.*)
ROSE. (*A warning.*) Yes, of course. Now, I know it will be bad for you, Ben, but since you're being so stubborn, I didn't know what else to do.

49

GRIGGS. (D. *to above chair* L. *of table. Approving.*) I think you *should* see Henry.

ROSE. But he's going to be very, very, very angry, Ben. And you know how much influence he has in Washington.

GRIGGS. (*Turns, carefully.*) Tell him to use his influence. And tell him to go to hell. (*Sips coffee.*)

ROSE. On a Sunday? (*Giggles.*)

GRIGGS. (*Crossing* R. *to above table. Gently.*) Rose, no years will make you serious.

ROSE. (*Slightly hurt.*) You used to like me that way.

GRIGGS. (*Bitter smile.*) So you always wanted to believe.

ROSE. How can I just walk in to Henry's happy house and say Ben wants a divorce, and I don't even know the reason? I *ask* him and I *ask* him but he says there is no reason ——

GRIGGS. (*Crossing to* R. *end of sofa.*) I never said there was no reason. But it isn't the reason that you like, or will accept. If I were in love with another woman you'd rather enjoy that. And certainly Henry would.

ROSE. It would at least be human. I've done a good deal of thinking about it, and I've just about decided it's why you stayed in Europe so long. (*Rises, crosses to* L. *of sofa.*) Henry said it at the time. (*Smiles.*) And you didn't guess that it was Henry who got you your last promotion.

GRIGGS. (*Not angry, but impatient.*) Rose, stop that. You're lying. You always do it about now. (*Crosses* R. *to above table, puts coffee down.*) Give Henry this reason: tell him my wife's too young for me.

ROSE. (*Not understanding. Hurt.*) I've wanted to stay young, I've ——

GRIGGS. (*Crossing* R. *to doors.*) You've done more than stay young: you've stayed a child.

ROSE. (*Starting to attack him.*) What about your mother, Ben, have you thought of her? It would kill her ——

GRIGGS. (*Slightly exasperated.*) She's been dead sixteen years.

ROSE. (*Crossing* R. *to above* R. *end of sofa.*) You know what I mean. She loved me and she was happy for our marriage.

GRIGGS. No, she didn't. She warned me not to marry ——

ROSE. (*Angrily.*) *Your* mother loved me. You have no right to malign the dead. I say she loved me, I know she did.

50

GRIGGS. (*Crossing* U. *to* U. C. *Wearily.*) What difference does it make?

ROSE. (*Crossing* L. *few steps.*) You never think anybody loves me. (*Turns back.*) Quite a few men have found me attractive ——

GRIGGS. (*Agreeing. Quickly.*) And many more will, my dear.

ROSE. (*A new tack. Crossing* R. *to below butler's tray.*) I always knew in the end I would have to tell you, although I haven't seen him since you came home. That I promise you. (*He crosses* R. *to* R. *windows.*) I told him you were a war hero with a glorious record and he said he wouldn't either any longer ——

GRIGGS. (*Who is at* R. *window. Hurriedly.*) Henry's chauffeur is outside, Rose.

ROSE. He was very, very, very, very much in love with me while he was at the Pentagon.

GRIGGS. (*Thrown away. With emphasis.*) Good place to be in love. The car is outside, Rose. (*Crosses* D. *to* L. *of lamp.*)

ROSE. (*Crossing to above chair* R. *of table.*) Even after we both knew it, he kept on saying that you didn't make love to a friend, more than a friend's, wife.

GRIGGS. (*Turns back to her.*) Rose, don't let's talk this way.

ROSE. Does it *hurt* you? Well, you've hurt me enough. The third time you went to Europe was when it really began. Because I, too, wanted affection.

GRIGGS. (*Gently.*) I can understand that.

ROSE. (*Starting to get hysterical.*) Ask me who it was. Ask me, Ben, and I will tell you. (*No answer.*) Just ask me.

GRIGGS. (*Crossing* D. R.) No, I won't do that, Rose.

ROSE. (*Crossing to* R. *of table.*) Remember when the roses came from Cairo, I mean wired from Cairo last birthday? That's who sent them. You didn't even like Cairo. You said it was filthy and the people down-trodden. But he sent roses.

GRIGGS. (*Crossing* L. *to below chair* L. *of table.*) He sounds like the right man. Go to him, Rose, the flying time is nothing now.

ROSE. (*Angrily*) You just stop being nasty. (*Slight pause. Crosses to him. Then, quietly with decision.*) And now I am going to tell you who it is.

GRIGGS. Please, Rose. We have had so many years of this—Please. (*Crosses* L. *to* D. R. *of sofa. As he is closer to him.*) Do I have to tell you that I don't care who it is?

ROSE. (*Crossing to him. She begins to move on him, in loud whis-*

per.) I'd like to whisper it. I knew if I ever told you I'd have to whisper it. (*Crosses* L., *sits chair* L. *of sofa. He begins now really to back away.*) Ben, you come right here. (*Crosses* L. *to above sofa. He starts to laugh.*) Stop that laughing. (*Very loudly, very close to him.*) It was your cousin, Ralph Sommers. There. (*She turns away.*) There. You won't ever speak with him about it? (*Crosses* R. *to* R. *of sofa.*)

GRIGGS. You can be sure of that.

ROSE. Oh, I'm late. I can't talk any more now, Ben. (*Exasperated.*) What am I going to tell Henry? Anyway, you know Henry isn't going to allow me to give you a divorce. You know that, Ben. (*Sweetly.*) And therefore I won't be able to do what you want, and the whole day is just wasted. Please tell me not to go, Ben.

GRIGGS. (*Rises, crossing* R. *to* D. R. *of sofa. As if he has held on to himself long enough.*) Tell Henry that I want a divorce. But in any case I am going away. I am leaving. That is all that matters to me or need matter to you or him. I would prefer a divorce. But I am going, whatever you and Henry decide. Understand that, Rose, the time has come to understand it.

ROSE. (*Thoughtfully, gently.*) I am going to try, dear. Really I am. It's evidently important to you. (*Crosses* U., *picks up overnight case by phone table. She exits through hall.* GRIGGS *sits down* L. *of table as if he were very tired. A minute later* CROSSMAN *comes from direction of dining-room, carrying Sunday papers. He looks at* BEN, *goes to him, hands him front page.* BEN *takes it, nods, sits holding it.* CROSSMAN *crosses to a chair* L. *of sofa, sits down, begins to read comic section. A second later* NINA *comes down stairs, comes into room, starts to speak to* BEN *and* CROSSMAN, *changes her mind and crosses up to phone chair, sits. Then* CONSTANCE, *in an old-fashioned flowered hat and carrying a large palmetto fan, comes through hall and into room.*)

CONSTANCE. I'm off to church. Anybody want anything just ring for Leon or Sophie. Want to come to church with me, Ned? (*He peers over his paper.*) All right. I just thought . . . Well, Nick told us that you told him last night . . .

CROSSMAN. I think perhaps I shall never again go out at night.

CONSTANCE. Oh, it's good for all of us to confide in somebody. (*She becomes conscious of* NINA *and* GRIGGS. *Smiles awkwardly, then with great determination leans over and kisses* CROSSMAN.) Good-bye, darling.

NINA. (*Rises, crosses* L. *upstage to between sofa and table. After a minute, hesitantly.*) I've got a car and a full picnic basket and a cold bottle of wine. Would you—(*Turning to* CROSSMAN, *then to* GRIGGS.) like to come along? I don't know where to go, but ——
CROSSMAN. (*Gaily.*) Got enough in your picnic basket for lunch *and* dinner?
NINA. (*Smiles.*) I think so.
CROSSMAN. Got a mandolin?
NINA. (*Smiles.*) No. Does that rule me out?
CROSSMAN. Almost. But we'll make do. The General whistles very well.
GRIGGS. (*Smiles, gets up.*) Is one bottle of wine enough on a Sunday?
NINA. (*Laughs as she goes toward hall.*) Not for the pure in heart. I'll get five or six more. (GRIGGS *slams papers on table, follows her out through hall.*)

CURTAIN

ACT II

SCENE 2

SCENE: *The same. Nine-thirty that evening.*

AT RISE: NICK *is lying on couch. He sips his drink. Next to him, on coffee table, is an empty champagne glass. On phone table, in a silver cooler, is a bottle of champagne.* CONSTANCE *is sitting at table playing solitaire and humming to the record on the phonograph. On porch* SOPHIE, *sitting* R. *of table, is reading to* MRS. ELLIS, *who is above table. Small tray with 4 champagne glasses on table by* CONSTANCE.

NICK. (*Looks up from couch, to* CONSTANCE, *irritably.*) Please don't hum.
CONSTANCE. Sorry. I always like that so much, I ——
NICK. And please don't talk. Handel doesn't need it.
CONSTANCE. Bach.

53

NICK. Handel.

CONSTANCE. (*Tartly.*) I'm sorry, but it's Bach.

NICK. (*Sits up. Takes glass from coffee table.*) You know damn well I know what I'm talking about. (*Drinks.*)

CONSTANCE. You don't know what you're talking about. Go look.

NICK. (*Gets up, picks up his glass, goes* U. L. *to phonograph, shuts it off, looks down, looks at her, she smiles. He turns away annoyed, picks up champagne bottle, then crosses* D. *to above table, brings bottle to* CONSTANCE. *Calling.*) Ready for another?

CONSTANCE. I haven't finished this. (NICK *carries bottle out to porch, crosses* D. *to above table.*)

MRS. ELLIS. (*As he offers her his glass, looks up at him.*) For the fourth time, we don't want any. Please go away. We're having a nice time. We're in the part I like best.

NICK. A nice time? Will I think such a time is a nice time when I am your age? I suppose so.

MRS. ELLIS. No, Nicholas. If you haven't learned to read at your age, you won't learn at mine.

NICK. (*Laughs, pats her shoulder.*) Never mind, I like you. (*Crosses* U. *few steps.*)

MRS. ELLIS. (*As he turns.*) You must be damn hard up. People seldom like those who don't like them.

NICK. (*Crossing* D. *to* MRS. ELLIS' R. *Smiling, but starting to be hurt.*) You haven't forgotten how to flirt. (*Grumbling.*) Come on inside and talk to me. (*Crosses* U. *to downstage door pillar.*) My wife disappears, everybody disappears —— (*Angry.*) I'm bored, I'm bored.

MRS. ELLIS. (*Rebuking him.*) And that's a state of sin, isn't it?

NICK. (*Almost to himself.*) Unfortunately, it isn't. I've always said I can stand any pain, any trouble—but not boredom.

MRS. ELLIS. (*As he crosses* D. *to her* R.) My advice is to try something intellectual for a change. Sit down with your champagne— on which you've been chewing since early afternoon—and try to make a paper hat out of the newspaper or get yourself a nice long bit of string.

NICK. (*Goes to* SOPHIE. *Pleading.*) Sophie, come in and dance with me.

MRS. ELLIS. (*Calls in.*) Constance, whistle for Mr. Denery, please. (CONSTANCE *looks up, then goes back to cards.*)

NICK. (*Reaching toward* SOPHIE.) You don't want to sit here and read to Mrs. Ellis.

SOPHIE. (*Settling more into chair.*) Yes, sir, I do. I enjoy the adventures of Ulysses. (*To* MRS. ELLIS.) *And* the dollar an hour Mrs. Ellis pays me for reading to her.

NICK. (*Consoling. Laughs, as* MRS. ELLIS *laughs.*) Give you two dollars an hour to *dance* with me.

MRS. ELLIS. It's not nearly enough, Sophie.

NICK. (*Pats* MRS. ELLIS *on* L. *shoulder.*) You're a corrupter of youth—you steal the best hours.

MRS. ELLIS. (*Knocks his hand off her shoulder.* NICK *crosses* R. *to* U. L. *of* SOPHIE. NICK *smiles but is slightly hurt.*) And you're a toucher: you constantly touch people or lean on them. Little moments of sensuality. One should have sensuality whole, or not at all. Don't you find pecking at it ungratifying? There are many of you: the touchers and the leaners. All since the depression, is my theory.

NICK. (*Smiles, pats her again.*) You must have been *quite* a girl in your day.

MRS. ELLIS. I wasn't. I wasn't at all. (NICK *wanders into room, to cooler, puts champagne in it after filling his glass, sits by phone.* MRS. ELLIS *speaks to* SOPHIE, *almost to herself.*) I was too good for those who wanted me and not good enough for those I wanted. (*To* SOPHIE.) Like Frederick, Sophie. Life can be hard for such people and they seldom understand why, and end bitter and confused.

SOPHIE. I know.

MRS. ELLIS. Do you? Frederick is a nice boy, Sophie—and that is all. But that's more than most, and precious in a small way.

SOPHIE. Yes, I think so. (MRS. ELLIS *smiles at* SOPHIE; SOPHIE *begins again to read.*)

NICK. (*Rises at phone table. Near phonograph, to* CONSTANCE.) Dance with me?

CONSTANCE. I don't know how any more.

NICK. (*Crossing* D. *to* D. R. *of sofa.*) Has it been wise, Constance, to lose all the graces in the service of this house?

CONSTANCE. Do you think I wanted it that way?

NICK. (*Crossing* L., *puts glass on coffee table, sits on* L. *end of sofa with feet up. Being truthful.*) I'm not sure you didn't. You

55

could have married Ned, instead of dangling him around, the way you've done.

CONSTANCE. Ned has come here each summer because, well, because I guess this is about the only home he has. I loved Ned and honored him, but *you'd* have been the first to tell me that you can't marry unless you're in love —— (*He begins to laugh. Angrily.*) Please don't laugh at me!

NICK. What are you so angry about? Want to know something? I've never been angry in my life. (*Turns to her, smiles.*) In the end, we wouldn't have worked out. You're a *good* woman and I am not a *good* man.

CONSTANCE. Well, whatever the reason, things turned out for the best. (*Carefully.*) About Ned. What did he say last night? I mean did he really talk about me?

NICK. (*Expansively.*) He said he loved you and wanted you and had wasted his life loving you and wanting you. And that he wasn't coming here any more. This is his last summer in this house.

CONSTANCE. (*Rises. She turns, pained, startled, crosses R.*) His last summer? He said that? He really said it was his last summer —— (CARRIE *comes quickly into room to above chair L. of table.*)

CARRIE. Has Fred come back?

NICK. (*Crossing around sofa to her.* CARRIE *crosses L. to porch after he crosses U. To her.*) Well, where have *you* been? (*Crosses U. to cooler, gets champagne.*) Come and have a drink and talk to me. (*He moves to pour her a drink as she crosses to porch.* NICK. *crosses D. to table, pours drink, leaves champagne on table.*)

CARRIE. (*Crossing D. to above table. Softly, to MRS. ELLIS.*) I've been everywhere. Everywhere possible. I even forced myself to call on Mr. Payson.

MRS. ELLIS. And what did he say? (SOPHIE *rises, crosses U., puts book on table, then crosses D. to D. L. of MRS. ELLIS.*)

CARRIE. That Fred came in to see him after he left here this morning, stayed a few minutes, no more, and he hasn't seen him since.

MRS. ELLIS. Ah, that's good.

CARRIE. What's good about it? It means we don't know where he's been since ten this morning. (NICK *crosses L. to porch with glass of champagne. Softly, as she sits down chair R. of table.*) I don't know what else to do or where else to look. What should

56

I do? Shall I call the police, what else is there to do? (CONSTANCE *sits again R. of table, resumes game of solitaire.*)

MRS. ELLIS. Nothing.

CARRIE. (*Rises, crossing U. to above her chair. Blaming herself, too.*) How can I do nothing? You shouldn't have made me threaten him. We were wrong. It wasn't important that he wanted to go to Europe with a man his own age. What harm was there in it?

MRS. ELLIS. (*Sharply.*) All his life you've been plucking him this way and plucking him that. Do what you like. Call the police.

NICK. (*Who has come to porch carrying glass for CARRIE. Crosses D. to above R. chair. He hears last few speeches, excited.*) Can I do anything, Carrie?

CARRIE. (*Crossing L. to him.*) I don't know, Nick. I only found one person who had seen him, down by the water ——

NICK. Is he—would he have—is that what you're thinking, Carrie? (*Quickly, the kind of efficient that comes with liquor and boredom.*) Then come on, Carrie. You must go to the police right away. I'll get a boat. Tell the police to follow along. Right away. (*Starts U. with CARRIE.*)

SOPHIE. (*Crossing U. to U. L. of chair above table. Angrily, in French, to NICK.*) [Do not enjoy the excitement so much. Stop being a fool.] *Ne profitez pas de cette excitation, ne faites pas l'imbécile.*

NICK. (*At L. of CARRIE. Amazed.*) What? (CONSTANCE *rises, crosses U., looking toward porch, then crosses D. Sits.*)

SOPHIE. (*In French.*) [I said don't enjoy yourself so much. Mind your business.] *Ne vous amusez pas tant, mêlez vous de vos affaires.*

CARRIE. (*Crossing L. to SOPHIE, takes her by the arm, whirls her R.*) What? What is it, Sophie?

SOPHIE. (*Between NICK and CARRIE. To CARRIE, slightly annoyed.*) Frederick is in the cove down by the dock. He has been there all day.

NICK. (*Crossing D. to above R. chair. Amazed, to SOPHIE.*) Don't you ever call me a fool again. I don't like such words, Sophie. I don't.

CARRIE. (*Sharply, to SOPHIE.*) You've let me go running about all day, frantic with terror ——

SOPHIE. He wanted to be alone, Mrs. Ellis. That is not so terrible a thing to want.

CARRIE. How dare you take this on yourself? How dare you ——
MRS. ELLIS. (*Sharply.*) I hope this is not a sample of you as a mother-in-law. (CARRIE *crosses* U. *few steps.*)
SOPHIE. (*Gently, to* CARRIE.) He will return, Mrs. Ellis. Leave him alone.
NICK. (*At behind* R. *chair. Softly grumbling, but more aware of her than before.*) Sophie, I think you owe me an apology. You are by way of being a rather sharp little girl underneath all that shyness, aren't you? I'm waiting. (*No answer.*) I'm waiting.
MRS. ELLIS. Well, wait outside, will you? (*He stares at her, turns, goes in the room.*)
NICK. (*Very hurt, to* CONSTANCE, *grumbling.*) I don't think I like it around here, Constance. No, I don't like it. (*He goes out* R. *windows as* CONSTANCE *stares at him.* SOPHIE *starts* U. *toward living-room.* CARRIE *stops her.*)
CARRIE. (*At* L. *of* SOPHIE.) Since Frederick has confided in you, Sophie, perhaps you should go to him.
SOPHIE. He has not confided in me. Sometimes his troubles are his own. (*She walks through room, sits* L. *of table, near* CONSTANCE, *who looks at her curiously. On porch,* CARRIE *crosses* D. R. *a step,* MRS. ELLIS *rises, crosses to* L. *of* CARRIE, *leans over and whispers to* CARRIE.)
CARRIE. Not tonight.
MRS. ELLIS. (*Crossing to living-room. Sharply.*) Why not tonight? We'll be leaving in the morning.
CARRIE. (*Following her.*) Because I've changed my mind. I think it best now that we let him go to Europe.
MRS. ELLIS. (*Stops above sofa.*) He will not want to go to Europe. Haven't you understood that much?
CARRIE. (*Hesitantly.*) How do you know what he wants or feels ——?
MRS. ELLIS. (*Crossing above sofa.*) I know. (*She comes in to room, crossing to* R. *end of sofa.* CARRIE *follows her in, stands below* L. *end of sofa.*) Sophie, I think a decision had best be made now. There should be no further postponement.
CARRIE. (*Very nervous.* L. *end of sofa.*) This isn't the time. Fred will be angry ——
MRS. ELLIS. (*Crossing* R. *to* SOPHIE. *To* SOPHIE, *who looks front, thinking.*) I don't want to push you, child, but nothing will change, nothing. I know you've wanted to wait, and so did Frederick, both

of you hoping that maybe —— But it will all be the same a year from now. Miracles don't happen. I'm telling you the truth, Sophie.

SOPHIE. (*Rises, crossing* D. R. *to* U. L. *of chair. Making a decision.*) Yes, Mrs. Ellis, and I agree with you. Nothing will change. If Frederick is willing for an early marriage, then I am also willing. (MRS. ELLIS *crosses to* U. L. *of* L. *chair.*)

CONSTANCE. (*Hurt—unbelieving.*) Is this the way it's been? (*Rises.*) Willing to marry, willing to marry ——

SOPHIE. (*Turns back to them. Looks at her.*) I do not use the correct word?

CONSTANCE. (*To* MRS. ELLIS *and* CARRIE.) If that's the way it is, then I am not willing. I thought it was two young people who—who loved each other. I didn't ever understand it, and I didn't ask questions, but —— Willing to get married! (*Accusingly*) What have you been thinking of, why —— (*To* CARRIE, *sharply, hurt.*) What kind of unpleasant thing has this been?

CARRIE. (*At above chair* L. *of sofa.*) I—I know. I can't ——

MRS. ELLIS. (*To* CONSTANCE *and* CARRIE.) Why don't you take each other by the hand and go outside and gather in the dew? (CARRIE *crosses to behind chair, faces* U. L. MRS. ELLIS *crosses, sits* R. *end of sofa, facing upstage, but watching scene.*)

CONSTANCE. (*Crossing* L. *to above table.* To SOPHIE, *sharply.*) When Carrie first talked to me about the marriage, I asked you immediately and you told me you were in love ——

SOPHIE. (*Surprised.*) I never told you that, Aunt Constance.

CONSTANCE. I don't remember your exact words, but of course I understood —— You mean you and Frederick have never been in love? Why? Then why have you ——?

SOPHIE. (*Crossing* U. *to above chair* R. *Trying to make her understand.*) Aunt Constance, I have not been happy, and I cannot continue here. I cannot be what you have wished me to be, and I do not want the world you want for me.

CONSTANCE. (*Softly.*) I've tried to give you everything ——

SOPHIE. I know what you have tried to give me, and I am grateful. But it has been a foolish waste for us both.

CONSTANCE. (*Softly.*) Were you happy at home, Sophie?

SOPHIE. (*Crossing* D. R. *to* L. *of chair* D. R. *Simply.*) I did not think in such words.

CONSTANCE. (*Crossing* D. *to* L. *of* SOPHIE.) Please tell me.

SOPHIE. I was . . . comfortable with myself, if that is what you mean, and I *am* no longer.
CONSTANCE. (*Gently, takes her shoulder.*) I have been so wrong. And so careless in not seeing it. Do you want to go home now?
SOPHIE. (*Turns away.*) No. My mother cannot —— Well, it is not that easy. I do not —— (*As if it were painful.*) I do not wish to go home now.
CONSTANCE. (*Puzzled.*) Why—why don't you?
SOPHIE. (*Turns to her. With feeling.*) Please do not talk of it any more. Please allow me to do what I wish to do, and know is best for me. (*Smiles.*) And don't look such a way. Frederick and I will have a nice life, we will make it so. (*Kisses* CONSTANCE'S *cheek. Exits into hall behind stairs.* FREDERICK *opens door in hall,* U. R.)
CARRIE. (*Sharply.*) Don't be too disturbed, Constance. (FREDERICK *appears in hallway.*) I have decided that Frederick should go to Europe and this time I am not going to allow any interference of any kind. (CONSTANCE *crosses* L. *below sofa to porch, sits chair upstage table.* FREDERICK *appears in hall, comes into room* U. C. *He is in his shirt sleeves.*)
FREDERICK. (*Depressed.*) I'm not going to Europe, Mother.
CARRIE. (*Crossing* U. *to* L. *of sofa. Turns to him.*) I have had a bad day. And I have thought of many things. I was mistaken and you were right. You must go wherever you want—however you want to go.
FREDERICK. I am not going, Mother. Payson made that very clear to me this morning.
MRS. ELLIS. (*Rises, crossing* R. *to above* D. R. *chair.*) Don't, Frederick! It's not necessary. I know.
FREDERICK. (*Crossing* D. *a step. Not angry but very hurt.*) But evidently Mother doesn't . . . Payson made it clear to me that I was not wanted, and never had been unless I supplied the money.
CARRIE. (*After a second.*) I —— Er —— I don't believe he meant that. (*Crosses* R. *two steps above sofa.*) You just tell him that it's all been a mistake and there will certainly be money for the trip. Just go right back and say that, Frederick —— (*Crosses* R. *to his* L.)
FREDERICK. (*Crossing* D., *sits* R. *end of sofa. Very sharply.*) Mother! I don't want to see him again! Ever.
CARRIE. (*Crossing* D. *to above them.*) You often imagine people

60

don't like you for yourself. *I'll* go and tell Mr. Payson that it's all fixed now ——

MRS. ELLIS. (*Crossing* R. *to above table.*) Carrie, you're an ass. (*To* FREDERICK. *Crosses* L. *to* U. L. *of chair* L. *of table.*) But I hope you haven't wasted today feeling bitter about Mr. Payson. You have no right to bitterness. No right at all. Why shouldn't Mr. Payson have wanted your money, though I must say he seems to have been rather boorish about not getting it? People like us should pay for the interest of people like him. (CARRIE *crosses* L. *slowly to* L. *of sofa.*) Why should they want us otherwise? I don't believe he ever pretended to feel anything else about you.

FREDERICK. (*Softly.*) No, he never pretended.

MRS. ELLIS. (*Crossing* L. *to him.*) Then understand that you've been the fool, and not he the villain. Take next week to be sad: a week's long enough to be sad in, if it's true sadness. Plenty long enough. (*Crosses* R. *to above chair* R. *of table.*)

FREDERICK. (*Smiles.*) All right, Grandma. I'll take a week. (SOPHIE *appears at hall door.*)

SOPHIE. (*Crossing* D. *to him. To* FREDERICK.) You have had no dinner? (*Puts out her hand.*) Then come. I have made a tray for you. (*He takes her hand, rises, goes out* U. L. *in hall.* CARRIE *starts toward hall.*)

MRS. ELLIS. (*Crossing* U., *looks at* CARRIE.) Are you going to interfere this time, Carrie? (*No answer. Gently.*) I hope not. (*She goes out upstairs.* CARRIE *stands for a moment above sofa.* CONSTANCE *crosses in to* L. *of sofa.*)

CARRIE. I don't like it, either.

CONSTANCE. (*Wearily.*) This whole marriage business sounds like the sale of a shore-front property. Well, maybe you all know what you're doing. (*Sits* L. *end of sofa.*)

CARRIE. (*Crossing to* L. *end of sofa.*) I don't know what I'm doing.

CONSTANCE. Why did you *want* the marriage, Carrie? I mean a month ago when you spoke to me ——

CARRIE. I don't even know that.

CONSTANCE. You always seem so clear about everything. And so strong. Even when we were girls. I envied you that, Carrie, and wanted to be like you.

CARRIE. (*Laughs.*) Clear and strong? I wish I could tell you what

61

I've missed and what I've wanted. Don't envy me, Con. (*She exits toward hall and staircase. As she does,* NICK *comes in* D. R. *doors. He is now a little more drunk than when he went out. He is carrying a branch from a bush.*)

NICK. (*Crossing to* R. *end of hall door.*) Come on out, Carrie. It's wonderful night. Take you for a sail.

CARRIE. (*Smiles.*) Good night, Nick.

NICK. (*Crossing* U. *to stairs. As she goes up steps, sincerely.*) I'm lonely, Carrie. I wouldn't leave you if you were lonely. (*When she doesn't answer, he looks around, sees* CONSTANCE *sitting on sofa, stands against* R. *side of hall door. After a second.*) I wish I wanted to go to bed with you, Con. I just can't want to. I don't know why. I just don't want it.

CONSTANCE. (*Rises, crossing* U. *around* L. *of sofa to above it. Disgusted.*) Stop talking that way. (*She gets up. He grabs her arm.*)

NICK. (*Crossing* L. *to her above sofa.*) Now you're angry again. (*Puts his arms around her.*) I'll sing you a lullaby. Will you like that?

CONSTANCE. (*Struggling to get away. Almost crying. Breaks away, crossing* R. *above sofa.*) Look, Nick, you've been rather a trial tonight. Do go to bed.

NICK. (*Crossing above sofa and* R. *to above table.*) I'm not going to bed. I'm lonely. I'm —— (*Phone rings.* CONSTANCE *goes to it.* NICK *pours himself glass of champagne at table. Puts branch on table.*)

CONSTANCE. Yes? General Griggs isn't in, Rose. Oh. Yes. Just a minute. (*To* NICK.) Rose Griggs wants to talk to *you.*

NICK. (*Irritated slightly.*) What's the matter, she got some new kind of trouble? (*Pours drink at table.*)

CONSTANCE. (*Annoyed.*) Do you want the call, or don't you?

NICK. Tell her I'm busy. (*Drinks.*)

CONSTANCE. (*In phone.*) He's busy drinking, Rose. Shall I leave a message for General Griggs? —— Oh. (*Puts phone down, annoyed.*) She says it's absolutely and positively urgent that she speak with *you.* Not her husband. Absolutely and positively. (*Exits through hall.* NICK *puts bottle and glass on table, goes to phone.*)

NICK. (*Slightly annoyed.*) Look here, my dear, don't be telling people you want to speak to me and not to your husband. Sounds awful. (*Laughs.*) Oh. A most agreeable doctor. Must get to know

62

him. (*Sits.*) Look, you don't have to convince me. Save it for your husband. Anyway, I once knew a woman with heart trouble and it gave her a nice color. You didn't go to the doctor to believe him —— (*Sighs, listens.*) All right, of course I'm sorry. It sounds jolly nice and serious, and I apologize. (*Listens. Rises.*) Oh. Well, that is kind of you. Yes, tell your brother I'd like to stay with him. Oh, by Friday, certainly. How old is your niece? Is she the one with the braces on her teeth? (NINA *appears from hall entrance, crosses D. to above D. R. chair. She is followed by* GRIGGS, *who is carrying picnic basket. He puts it U. R., stands at R. end of hall door.* NICK, *sincerely angry.*) No, I won't paint anything out. That big a hack I'm not. (*Pleasanter.*) Yes, we'll have plenty of time together. You're a good friend. (*To* NINA *and* GRIGGS. *Affably.*) Had a nice day? (*Into phone.*) No, I'm talking to your husband. Oh. Goodbye. Take care of yourself. (*Hangs up. To* GRIGGS. *Jaunting.*) That was Rose. (*Gaily, to* NINA, *crossing D. to R. of sofa.*) I've had a dull day, darling. (GRIGGS *crosses L. to L. of sofa.* CROSSMAN *comes in.*) Where'd you skip to?

NINA. We drove over to Pass Christian.

NICK. Did you put the car in the garage?

CROSSMAN. (*Crossing D. to above table, puts keys on table.*) Yes, all safe.

NICK. Did you drive, Ned? That heavy Isotta? (*To* NINA.) Nobody who drinks as much as Ned should be driving that car. (*Turns L. to* GRIGGS.) Or any car belonging to me.

NINA. (*Sharply.*) And nobody as tight as you are should talk that way. (NICK *crosses R. to L. of table, gets champagne, pours drink.*)

NICK. (*Apologizing to* NED. *Laughs.*) Have a drink, Ned. (*He brings* CROSSMAN *a glass.*)

CROSSMAN. Thank you, no. (NICK *turns toward* GRIGGS, *crosses to above sofa.*)

GRIGGS. (*At U. L. of sofa.*) No, thank you.

NICK. What the hell is this? Refusing to have a drink with me —— (*To* CROSSMAN.) I'm trying to apologize to you. (*Crosses to R. of sofa.*) Now take the drink ——

NINA. (*Sharply.*) Nick, please ——

NICK. Stay out of it, Nina. Women don't know anything about the etiquette of drinking.

CROSSMAN. (*Laughs. Bitterly.*) Has it got etiquette now? (*As

63

NICK *again hands him glass.* CROSSMAN *shakes his head.*) Thank
you.

NICK. (*Drunk, hurt.*) Look here, old boy, I say in the light of
what's happened, you've just got to take this. It's my way of
apologizing and I shouldn't have to explain that to a gentleman.
(*He grabs* CROSSMAN'S *arm, playfully presses glass to* CROSSMAN'S
*lips with his* L. *hand.*)

CROSSMAN. (*Takes* NICK'S L. *wrist with his* R. *hand. Quietly.*)
Don't do that.

NICK. Come on, old boy. If I have to pour it down you ——

CROSSMAN. Don't do that. (NICK, *laughing, presses glass hard
against* CROSSMAN'S *mouth.* CROSSMAN *pushes glass, which falls to
floor. He looks at* NINA, *then crosses* R.)

NINA. (*Sits down* R. *of table.*) Well, we got rid of that glass. But
there are plenty more, Nick.

NICK. (*Sad, but firm, to* CROSSMAN.) Now *you've* put *yourself*
on the defensive, my friend. (*Crosses* L. *to above sofa.*) That's
always tactically unwise, isn't it, General Griggs?

GRIGGS. I know nothing of tactics, Mr. Denery. Certainly not of
yours.

NICK. (*Jovially.*) Then what the hell are you doing as a general?

GRIGGS. (*Crossing* D. R. *to chair. Trying to be jolly.*) Masquerading.
They had a costume left over and they lent it to me.

NICK. (*To* CROSSMAN.) I'm waiting, Ned. Pour yourself a drink,
and make *your* apologies. (CROSSMAN *crosses* L. *to* NICK *as though
he might hit him. Pauses, turns, picks up glass.*)

CROSSMAN. (*Coldly angry.*) You are jus* exactly the way I remember you. (*Crosses* U., *turns in door.*) And that I wouldn't
have believed of any man. (*He turns, goes out* U. L. *in hall.*)

NICK. (*Crossing* U. *few steps. Like a hurt child.*) What the hell
does that mean? (*Calling.*) Hey, Ned. Come on back and have it
your way. (*Crosses to above table. Gets no answer, turns, pleading.*) Come on, General. Have a bottle with me. (*Pours drink,
takes glass and bottle, crosses* L. *to below phone table.*)

NINA. (*Wearily.*) Are we going to start again?

NICK. General, got something to tell you: your wife telephone
but she didn't want to speak to you.

GRIGGS. (*Crossing* R. *above sofa and below* NICK *to hall door.*)
That's most understandable. Good night, Mrs. Denery, and thank
you for a pleasant day.

64

NICK. But she'll want to speak to you in the morning. Better stick around in the morning.

GRIGGS. (*Stares at him.*) Thank you. Good night.

NICK. (*Following him.*) I think you're doing the wrong thing, wanting to leave Rose. You going to be lonely at your age without ——

GRIGGS. (*Crossing a step toward him. With dignity.*) If my wife wishes to consult you, Mr. Denery, that's her business. But I don't wish to consult you. (*He exits up stairs.*)

NICK. (*Crossing U. to stairs.*) Sorry. Forget it. (*Crosses L. to phone table, puts glass and bottle on it. Then crosses D., lies on sofa.*)

NINA. (*Almost to herself, after a pause.*) You know, it's a nasty business hating yourself.

NICK. Who's silly enough to do that?

NINA. (*Sharp.*) Me.

NICK. (*Raising himself on elbow. Warmly.*) Come on over here, darling, and tell me about yourself. I've missed you.

NINA. (*Still almost to herself.*) To hate yourself, all the time.

NICK. I love you, Nina.

NINA. (*Gets up. Crosses R. around above table, then L. to sofa, sits on R. end of it.*) Here we go with that routine. Now you'll bait me until I tell you that you've never loved any woman, or any man, nor ever will. (*Wearily.*) I'll be glad to get out of this house before Constance finds you out. She can go back to sleeping with her dreams. (*After a second.*) You still think you can wind up everybody's affairs by Friday?

NICK. (*Lies back, looking at ceiling.*) Oh, sure. Friday. Then we're going up to spend a month with Rose's brother, Henry something or other. In New Orleans.

NINA. What are you talking about?

NICK. Rose fixed it for me. I'm going to do a portrait of her niece, the heiress to the fortune. The girl is balding and has braces. Five thousand dollars.

NINA. Are you crazy?

NICK. Not a bit.

NINA. (*Referring to painting.*) It's all right for you to kid around here ——

NICK. (*Raising himself on his elbow.*) I *don't* know what you mean.

65

NINA. (*Rises, crosses* R. *to* L. *of chair* L. *of table. Violently.*)
Please don't let's talk this way. Just tell Mrs. Griggs that you've
changed your mind ——
NICK. (*Sits up, feet above sofa.*) I demand that you tell me what
you mean.
NINA. (*Angrily.*) How many years have we avoided saying it?
Why must you walk into it now? (*Crosses to* R. *of sofa. Pauses,
looks at him, hating to have to say it.*) All right. Maybe it's time:
you haven't finished a portrait in twelve years. And money isn't
your reason for wanting to do this portrait. You're setting up a
silly flirtation with Mrs. Griggs. I'm not going to New Orleans,
Nick. I am not going to watch it all again. I can't go on this way
for myself —— (*Sits* R. *end of sofa, feet in front. Then softly.*)
Don't go. Call it off. You know how it will end. Please let's don't
this time —— We're not young any more, Nick. Somewhere we
must have learned something.
NICK. (*Controlling his anger. Softly, carefully.*) If I haven't
finished every picture I started it's because I'm good enough to
know they weren't good enough. All these years you never understood that? I think I will never forgive you for talking that way.
NINA. (*Rises, backing to* R. *of sofa. Not being nasty.*) Like all
amateurs you have very handsome reasons for what you do not
finish.
NICK. (*Rises slowly above sofa.*) You have thought that about me,
all these years?
NINA. (*Emphatically.*) Yes.
NICK. (*Sarcastically.*) Then it was good of you and loyal to pretend you believed in me.
NINA. (*Crossing to him above sofa.*) Good? Loyal? What do they
mean? I loved you.
NICK. (*Turns* L.) Yes, good and loyal. But I, too, have a little
pride —— (*Turns back.* NINA *crosses* R. *to above table.*) And no
man can bear to live with a woman who feels that way about his
work. I think you ought to leave tomorrow, Nina. For good and
forever. (NINA *turns. A pause.*)
NINA. (*Softly, stunned.*) Yes. (*She turns.*) Yes, of course. (*She
starts to exit. He follows behind her, talking. She stops* U. C.)
NICK. But it must be different this time. Remember I said years
ago, "Ten times of threatening is out, Nina," I said—the tenth
time you stay gone.

NINA. (*Turns back to him. Quietly.*) All right. Ten times is out. (*Quietly, desperately.*) I promise for good and forever. (*Exits upstairs.*)

NICK. (*As she is climbing staircase.*) This time, spare yourself the return. And the begging and the self-humiliation and the self-hate. And the disgusting self-contempt. This time they won't do any good. (*He is following her, but we cannot see him. Starts up.*) Let's write it down, darling. And have a drink to seal it. (*On the words "disgusting self-contempt,"* CONSTANCE *comes into hall. She hears the words, recognizes* NICK'S *voice and stands, frowning and thoughtful. Then closes porch door, turns off porch light, comes back into living-room and begins to empty ash-trays on coffee table, table* R. C. *and* D. R.*; turns lamp off* D. R. *Empties ash-tray on phone table, turns out chandelier lights, etc.* SOPHIE *follows her into room carrying pillow, sheets, quilts, book, puts them on chair* L. *of sofa, a glass of milk, puts it on coffee table, and crosses to couch. Without speaking,* CONSTANCE *moves to help her, putting silent butler on phone table, together they begin to make couch for night.*)

SOPHIE. (*At above sofa. After a moment, smiles.*) Do not worry for me, Aunt Constance.

CONSTANCE. (*At* L. *end of sofa.*) I can't help it.

SOPHIE. I think perhaps you worry sometimes in order that you should not think.

CONSTANCE. (*Smiles.*) Yes, maybe. I won't say any more. I'll be lonely without you, Sophie. I don't like being alone, any more. It's not a good way to live. And with you married, I'll be alone forever, unless —— Well, Ned's loved me and it's been such a waste, such a waste. (*Stops making bed.* SOPHIE *continues.*) I know it now but—well—I don't know. (*Shyly, as a young girl would say it. Crosses to above sofa.*) I wanted you to understand, in case I came to a decision about us. (SOPHIE *looks at her.*) You understand, Sophie? (SOPHIE *stares at her, frowning.* CONSTANCE *kisses her cheek. Then* CONSTANCE *speaks happily.*) Sleep well, dear. (*Crosses* U. *Picks up silent butler, turns out bracket lights, exits, closing door.* SOPHIE *finishes with bed, takes off her robe, puts it around her shoulders, gets into bed, starts to read, then lies quietly, thinking. Then turns as she hears footsteps in hall, and she is staring at door as* NICK *opens it. He trips over threshold, recovers himself.*)

67

NICK. (*Sharply. At* D. R. *of phone table.*) Constance! What is this, a boys' school with lights out at eleven! (*Turns on wall brackets, pours drink. He sees* SOPHIE.) Where's your aunt? I want to talk to her. What are you doing?

SOPHIE. (*Wanting him to go away.*) I think I am asleep, Mr. Denery.

NICK. You're cute. Maybe too cute. (*Takes a sip. Puts glass on phone table.*) I'm going down to the tavern and see if I can get up a beach party. Tell your aunt. Just tell her that. (*Crosses* R. *to doors. Turns back.*) Want to come? (*Crosses* L. *to above chair* L. *of table.*) You couldn't be more welcome. (*Crosses to* R. *of sofa.*) Oh, come on. Throw on a coat. I'm not mad at you any more. (*He looks down at her.*) I couldn't paint you, Sophie. You're too thin. Damn shame you're so thin. (*Suddenly sits down* R. *end of sofa. Weary.*) I'm sick of trouble. Aren't you? Like to drive away with me for a few days? (*Smiles at her.*) Nobody would care. And we could be happy. I hate people not being happy. (*He lies down. His head is now on her knees.*) Move your knees, baby, they're bony. And get me a drink.

SOPHIE. (*Pulls her knees up.*) Take the bottle upstairs, Mr. Denery.

NICK. Get me a drink. And make it poison. (*Slowly, wearily, she gets up, puts book on coffee table, goes to bottle, pours drink. He begins to sing. She brings glass back to him. He reaches up to take glass, and spills the liquid on the bed.*) Clumsy, honey, clumsy. But I'll forgive you. (*Takes glass, puts it on coffee table, then puts arms around her. She pulls away. He is holding her around waist and laughing.*)

SOPHIE. (*Pulls away, crossing* R. *to above table. Calmly.*) Please go somewhere else, Mr. Denery.

NICK. (*Springs up, crossing* R. *to her. Drunk-angry.*) People aren't usually rude to me, Sophie. (SOPHIE *backs a step away.*) Poor little girls always turn rude when they're about to marry rich little boys. What a life you're going to have! (*Crosses to her.*) That boy doesn't even know what's the matter with him ——

SOPHIE. (*Very sharply.*) Please, Mr. Denery, go away.

NICK. (*Laughs.*) Oh, you *know* what's the matter with him? No European would be as innocent of the world as you pretend. (*Delighted. Touches her cheeks.*) I tricked you into telling me. Know that?

SOPHIE. (*Crossing* L. *above him to* R. *of sofa. Long-suffering.*) You are drunk and I am tired. Please go away.

NICK. Go to sleep, child. (*Crosses* D. R.) I'm not disturbing you. (*Sits down across the room.*) Go to sleep. (*She stares at him, decides she can't move him, crosses down stage to chair* L. *of sofa, picks up book, sits chair, begins to read.*) I won't say a word. (*He gets up, comes to above* U. L. *of bed, stands near her, speaking over her shoulder.*) Ssh. Sophie's reading. Do you like to read? Know the best way to read? With someone you love. Out loud. Ever try it that way, honey? I used to know a lot of poetry. Brought up on Millay. My candle, and all that. "I had to be a liar. My mother was a leprechaun, my father was a friar." Crazy for the girl. (*Leans over, kisses her hair tenderly. She pulls her head away. Romantic, tender. Backs upstage to phone table.*) Ever wash your hair in champagne, darling? I knew a woman once. (*Gets bottle. Crosses* D. *to above her, tips bottle over her head.*) Let's try it.

SOPHIE. (*Rises, puts book on coffee table. Sharply.*) Let us not try it again.

NICK. (*Crossing* R. *above sofa around to in front of* C. *of it. Sits down. Puts bottle on coffee table. Almost crying.*) Now for God's sake don't get angry. (*Takes her arms, shakes her.*) I'm sick of angry women. All men are sick of angry women, if angry women knew the truth.

SOPHIE. (*Backs away to* L. *of sofa.*) Mr. Denery, I am sick of you.

NICK. (*Withdraws slowly. Sad. Softly.*) Tell me you don't like me and I will go away and not come back.

SOPHIE. (*Crossing to* D. L. *of sofa.*) No, sir. I do not like you.

NICK. (*Can't believe it.*) People have hated me. But nobody's ever not liked me. If I didn't think you were flirting, I'd be hurt. If you kiss me, Sophie, be kind to me for just a minute, I'll go away. I may come back another day, but I'll go all by myself —— (*Takes her hand, desperately.*) Please, Sophie, please.

SOPHIE. (*As he takes her in his arms, pulls her to him. Struggles to get away from him. She speaks angrily.*) Do not make yourself such a clown. (*When she cannot get away from him.*) I will call your wife, Mr. Denery.

NICK. (*Delighted. Whispers loudly.*) That would be fun, go ahead. We're getting a divorce. Sophie, let's make this night our night. God, Cecile, if you only knew what I've been through ——

69

SOPHIE. (*Violently.*) Oh shut up. (*She pulls away from him with great effort, crosses* L. *to above chair* L. *of sofa. He catches her robe and rolls over on it.*)

NICK. (*Giggles as he settles down comfortably.*) Come on back. It's nice and warm here and I love you very much. But we've got to get some sleep, darling. Really we have to. (*Then he turns over and lies still. She stands looking at him.*)

SOPHIE. (*After a moment, alarmed.*) Get up, Mr. Denery. I will help you upstairs. (*No answer. Crosses to* L. *of sofa.*) Please, please get up.

NICK. (*Gently, half passed-out.*) It's raining out. Just tell the concierge I'm your brother. She'll understa —— (*The words fade off.* SOPHIE *waits a second, then leans over and with great strength begins to shake him, turns him.*) Stop that. (*He passes out, begins to breathe heavily. She turns, walks to hall door, stands there. Then changes her mind, comes back into room. She goes to couch, stands looking at him, decides to pull him by the legs. Softly.*) I'll go away in a few minutes. (*She drops his legs.*) Don't be so young. Have a little pity. I am old and sick. (*SOPHIE crosses* L., *gets blanket from chair* L. *of sofa, puts blanket around shoulders, crosses slowly* D. R., *sits as curtain falls.*)

## CURTAIN

## ACT III

SCENE: *Seven o'clock the next morning.* NICK *is asleep on couch.* SOPHIE *is sitting in a chair,* R. *of table facing front, drinking cup of coffee. A moment after rise of curtain,* MRS. ELLIS *comes down steps, comes into room.*

MRS. ELLIS. (*Crossing* D. *toward table.*) I heard you bumping around in the kitchen, Sophie. The older you get the less you sleep, and the more you look forward to meals. Particularly breakfast, because you've been alone all night, and the nights are the hardest —— (*Crosses to* R. *of sofa. She sees* NICK, *stares, moves over to look at him.*) What is this?

SOPHIE. It is Mr. Denery. (*Sips coffee.*)

MRS. ELLIS. (*Turns to stare at her.*) What's he doing down here?

SOPHIE. He became drunk and went to sleep.

MRS. ELLIS. He has been here all night? (*Crosses* R. *to above table.* SOPHIE *nods.*) What's the matter with you? Get him out of here immediately.

SOPHIE. (*Rises, crossing around to above chair* R. *of table.*) I cannot move him. I tried. Shall I get you some coffee?

MRS. ELLIS. (*Staring at her.*) Are you being silly, Sophie? Sometimes it is very hard to tell with you. Why didn't you call Constance or Mrs. Denery?

SOPHIE. (*As* MRS. ELLIS *crosses* L. *to above sofa.*) I did not know what to do. Mr. and Mrs. Denery had some trouble between them, or so he said, and I thought it might be worse for her if —— (*Smiles.*) Is it so much? He was just a little foolish and sleepy. (*Goes toward door.*) I will get Leon and Sadie and we will take him upstairs.

MRS. ELLIS. (*Grabs* SOPHIE, *stops her.*) You will not get Leon and Sadie. Rose Griggs may be President of the gossip club for summer Anglo-Saxons, but Leon is certainly President of the Negro chapter. (*Crosses back to above sofa.*) You will get this, er, out of here before anybody else sees him. (*She is above bed, pulls blanket off* NICK.) At least he's dressed. Bring me that cup of coffee. (SOPHIE *brings cup from table to her.*) Nicholas! Sit

71

up! (NICK *moves his head slightly. To* SOPHIE.) Hold his head up. (SOPHIE *crosses to* L. *of sofa.* SOPHIE *holds* NICK'S *head,* MRS. ELLIS *tries to make him drink.*)

NICK. (*Very softly.*) Please leave me alone.

MRS. ELLIS. (*Shouting in his ear.*) Nicholas, listen to me! *You are to get up and get out of here immediately.*

NICK. (*Giving a bewildered look around the room, then closes his eyes.*) Cecile.

SOPHIE. (MRS. ELLIS *gives* SOPHIE *coffee cup.*) He has been speaking of Cecile most of the night. (*Puts cup on coffee table, crosses back to* U. L. *of sofa.*)

MRS. ELLIS. (*Very sharply.*) Shall I wake your wife and see if she can locate Cecile for you, or would you rather be cremated here? Get up, Nicholas. (*He opens his eyes, shuts them again.*)

SOPHIE. You see how it is? (*She tries to pull her robe from under him.*) Would you get off my robe, Mr. Denery?

MRS. ELLIS. Sophie, you're a damned little ninny. (*Very loud to* NICK.) Now get up. You have no right to be here. You must get up immediately. I say *you*, you get up! (*Shouting.*) Get to your room. Get out of here.

NICK. (*Turns, opens his eyes, half sits up, speaks gently.*) Don't scream at me, Mrs. Ellis. (*Sees* SOPHIE, *begins to realize where he is, groans deeply.*) I passed out?

SOPHIE. (*Almost sympathetically.*) Yes, sir. Most deeply. (NICK *lies back.*)

MRS. ELLIS. I'm sure after this he won't mind if you don't call him "sir." (*Crosses* R. *then back to above sofa.*)

NICK. Champagne's always been a lousy drink for me. How did I get down here? (*Turns head down stage to* SOPHIE.) I'm sorry, child. What happened?

SOPHIE. (*Crossing* D. *to* D. L. *of sofa.*) You fell asleep.

NICK. (*Hesitantly.*) Did I—God, I'm a fool! What did I —— Did I do anything or say anything? Tell me, Sophie. (*Lies back.* MRS. ELLIS *crosses* R.) I'm thirsty. I want a quart of water. Or a bottle of beer. Get me a bottle of cold beer, Sophie, will you? (*Rises up again. Looks around bed.*) Where'd you sleep? (*Lies back.*) Get me the beer, will you? (SOPHIE *crosses* U., *steps to* U. L. *of sofa, looks at* MRS. ELLIS, *who signals her not to.*)

MRS. ELLIS. (*Crossing* L. *to* U. R. *of sofa. Carefully.*) Nicholas, you are in Sophie's bed, in the living-room of a house in a small

72

southern town where for a hundred and fifty years it has been impossible to take a daily bath without everybody in town advising you not to dry out your skin. You know that as well as I do. Now get up and go out by the side lawn, and come back through the front door for breakfast. (*Crosses* R. *few steps.*)

NICK. I couldn't eat breakfast.

MRS. ELLIS. (*Crossing* L. *to* R. *end of sofa.*) I don't find you cute. I find only that you can harm a young girl. Do please understand that.

NICK. Yes, I do. And I'm sorry. (*He sits up, untangling himself from robe.*) What's this? Oh, Sophie, child, I must have been a nuisance. I am *so* sorry.

MRS. ELLIS. (*Very loudly.*) Get up and get the hell out of here. (*Door opens* D. R. *and* ROSE, *carrying her overnight handbag, sticks her head in, enters, leaves doors open.*)

ROSE. (*To* MRS. ELLIS, *who is directly on a line with door. At* D. R. *door.*) You frightened me. (*Crosses* L. *to above table.*) I could hear you outside on the lawn, so early. (*Puts bag by chair upstage of door.*) Oh, Nick. How nice you're downstairs. (*Crosses* L. *to* L. *of table. Her voice trails off as she sees* SOPHIE *and realizes* NICK *is on bed.*) Oh. (*Crosses to* D. C. *Giggles, hesitantly.*) You look like you just woke up, Nick. (*Backs away* R. *to below chair* R. *of table.*) I mean, just woke up where you are.

MRS. ELLIS. (*Crossing* U. *few steps. To* NICK.) Well, that's that. (*Crosses* D. *to* U. R. *of sofa.*) Perhaps you wanted it this way, Nicholas. (*She starts out as* LEON *appears carrying coffee urn.* ROSE *stands staring at* NICK.)

LEON. (*At* R. *end of hall door. Very curious, but very hesitant in doorway.*) Should I put it here this morning, like every day, or ——?

MRS. ELLIS. Who told you, Leon?

LEON. (*Obviously lying. Trying to look over her shoulder at* NICK.) Told me what, Mrs. Ellis? Sadie says take on in the coffee ——

MRS. ELLIS. I'm not talking about the coffee. Who told you about Mr. Denery being here?

LEON. Told me? Why, Miss Sophie came in for coffee for them.

MRS. ELLIS. (*To* SOPHIE.) Why didn't you tell me that? Did you think I needed the exercise of getting him out of bed? If they heard it in the kitchen an hour ago the news has reached Tidewater- Maryland by now. (*After a second, shrugs, points to coffee.*) Take it into the dining-room.

LEON. You want me come back and straighten up, Miss Sophie?

MRS. ELLIS. (*Looks at* MRS. GRIGGS, *crosses* U.) Mrs. Griggs will be glad to straighten up. (*She exits.* LEON *follows her out.*)

ROSE. (*Crossing* L. *below table to below coffee table, back* R. *to below table. Softly to* NICK, *shocked.*) You were here all night? I come back needing your help and advice as I've never before needed anything. And I find you ——

NICK. Rose, please stop moving about. You're making me seasick. And would you go outside? I'd like to speak to Sophie.

ROSE. (*Crossing* L. *to* U. R. *of sofa.*) I am waiting for you to explain, Nick. I don't understand.

NICK. (*Irritated.*) There is no need for you to understand.

ROSE. But please tell me, Nick, what happened and then I won't be angry.

NICK. (*Annoyed.*) What the hell are you talking about? What's it your business? Now go upstairs, Rose.

ROSE. (*Softly, indignant.*) "Go upstairs, Rose." "What's it your business?" After I work my head off getting the commission of the portrait for you and after I go to the doctor's on your advice, although I never would have gone if I had known, and I come back here and find you this way. (*Sits down chair* L. *of table.*) You've hurt me and you picked a mighty bad day to do it. (CONSTANCE *comes in from hall. She goes to* NICK, *stands looking at him.*)

CONSTANCE. (*Crossing* D. *to* U. R. *of sofa.*) Nick, I want you to go to that window and look across the street. (*He stares at her. Then he gets up slowly and slowly moves* R. *to window* D. R. CONSTANCE *crosses* R. *to above chair* R. *of table.* SOPHIE *crosses* R. *to above sofa.*) The Carters have three extra guests on their breakfast porch, the Gable sisters are unexpectedly entertaining —— (*With feeling.*) This house was not built to be stared at.

NICK. (*Gently.*) It can't be that bad, Constance.

CONSTANCE. It is just that bad. (SOPHIE *crosses* L. *to* L. *of sofa.*)

NICK. (*Contrite.*) I'm sorry. I was silly and drunk but there's no sense making more out of it than that.

CONSTANCE. I am not making *anything* out of it. But I know what is *being* made out of it. (NICK *crosses* D. R., *sits.*) In your elegant way of life, I daresay this is an ordinary occurrence. But not in

74

our village. Please explain to me what happened. (*Points to phone, then across street.*) I only know what they know.

SOPHIE. (*Factually.*) Mr. Denery came down looking for someone to talk to. He saw me, recited a little poetry, spoke to me of his troubles, tried to embrace me in a most mild fashion. (ROSE *turns, points to* NICK.) And fell into so deep a sleep that I could not move him. Alcohol. It is the same in my country, every country. (SOPHIE *puts pillow on chair* L. *of sofa.* ROSE *puts head in hand, leaning on table.*)

CONSTANCE. (*Softly, as if it pained her.*) You are taking a very light tone about it, Sophie, a shocking light tone.

SOPHIE. I will speak whichever way you think most fits the drama, Aunt Constance. (*Refusing to quarrel. Crosses to above sofa, picks up robe, crosses* L. *down stage.*)

CONSTANCE. Will you tell me why you stayed in the room? Why didn't you come and call me, or ——?

NICK. (*Rises, crossing around and above table to* C.) Oh, look here. It's obvious. The kid didn't want to make any fuss and thought I'd wake up and go any minute. (*Sincerely.*) Damn nice of you, Sophie, and I'm grateful. Look. A foolish guy drinks, passes out —— (*Crosses* U. *into hall, fixes tie, combs hair.*)

ROSE. (*Amazed as she turns to look at* SOPHIE.) Why, look at Sophie. Just as calm as can be. Making the bed. Like it happened to her every night.

CONSTANCE. (*Turns, realizes* ROSE *is in room. Crosses* D. *to* D. R. *of chair* R. *of table.*) What are you doing here?

ROSE. Sitting here thinking that no man sleeps in a girl's bed unless she gives him to understand —— (CONSTANCE *stares at her.*) You can blame Nick all you like. But you know very well that a nice girl would have screamed.

CONSTANCE. (*Crossing to below chair* R. *of table.*) How dare you talk this way? Whatever gave you the right —— I hope it will be convenient for you to leave today. I will apologize to the General. (*Crosses* R. *to above chair* D. R. SOPHIE *puts bedclothes and pillow on chair* L. *of sofa.*)

ROSE. (*Softly.*) That's all right, Constance. (*Rises, crosses to above chair* L. *of table.*) I must leave today, in any case. You see, I have to —— (*Sighs, sincerely.*) You won't be mad at me for long when you know the story. Oh, I'm very tired now. Couldn't I have my breakfast in bed? Doctor's orders. (*Turns* U. *She goes*

75

*out, passes* CROSSMAN, *who is coming in, to* L. *of hall door. In sepulchral tones.*) Good morning, dear Ned. (*At* R. *of hall door. Then in a sudden burst.*) Have you heard ——?

CROSSMAN. (*Not being sarcastic.*) Good morning. Yes, I've heard. I'm not the one deaf man in town. (*Crosses* D. *to* L. *of chair* L. *of table.* SOPHIE *crosses* U., *gets sofa pillows from phone chair, puts them on sofa. He passes* ROSE. *She stares at his back, reluctantly exits.*)

CONSTANCE. (*Turns. Desperately.*) Ned, what should we do?

CROSSMAN. (*At chair* L. *of table.* NICK *crosses* D., *sits* R. *of sofa. Seriously.*) Is there always something that can be done, remedied, patched, pulled apart and put together again? There is nothing to "do," Con. (*Sits* L. *of table. Smiles to* SOPHIE, *amused.*) How are you, Sophie?

SOPHIE. (*At chair* L. *of sofa.*) I am all right, Mr. Ned.

NICK. Ned, is it as bad as (*Gestures toward window and* CONSTANCE.) Constance *thinks?*

CONSTANCE. (*Crossing to above table. Very angrily. Bitterly.*) You came here as my friend and in our small life—in our terms— you have dishonored my house. It has taken me too many years to find out that you ——

CROSSMAN. (*Trying to calm her.*) All right, Con, maybe that's the truth; but what's the good of discussing Nick's character and habits now?

NICK. (*Rises. Sincerely, to* CONSTANCE.) Whatever you think of me, I didn't want this. I know what it will mean to Sophie and I'll stay here and face anything that will help you. Anything I can say or do —— (*Crosses* U. *to phone chair, sits.*)

SOPHIE. (*Crossing* R. *to above coffee table. She has finished folding clothes. Has them in her arms.*) What *will* it "mean" to me, Mr. Ned?

CONSTANCE. (*Reproving.*) You're old enough to know. And I believe you do know.

SOPHIE. (*Crossing* R. *to* U. R. *of coffee table.*) I want to know from Mr. Ned what he thinks.

CROSSMAN. (*Rises, crossing to* D. R. *of sofa. To* SOPHIE.) I *know* what you want to know: the Ellis name is a powerful name. They won't be gossiped about out loud. They won't *gossip* about you and they won't listen to *gossip* about you. In their *own way* they'll take care of things. You can be quite sure of that. Quite sure.

76

SOPHIE. (*After a second.*) And that is all?

CROSSMAN. That is all.

SOPHIE. (*Softly.*) Thank you, Mr. Ned. (SOPHIE *crosses around L. of sofa, exits upstage of porch.*)

CONSTANCE. (*Puzzled and indignant.*) Take care of things? She hasn't done anything. Except be stupid. The Tuckerman name is as good as the Ellis name ——

CROSSMAN. (*Crossing R. to her above table.*) Yes, yes. Sure enough. (CONSTANCE *crosses toward stairs. Stops at foot of stairs. Sees* LEON *in hall. He is carrying his hat and crossing toward door R. She calls "LEON."*)

LEON. (*Crossing back into R. end of hall door.* CROSSMAN *crosses U. R.*) Mrs. Ellis is cutting up about her breakfast. And Sadie's waiting for orders. We're messed this morning, for good.

CONSTANCE. Not at all. Tell Sadie I'm coming. What's your hat for, Leon?

LEON. Well, kind of a hot sun today.

CONSTANCE. Not in here. Rest your hat: you'll have plenty of time to gossip when the sun goes down. (*Puts phone on hook.* LEON *and she go out U. L. in hall.* CROSSMAN *crosses L. few steps.*)

NICK. (*Miserably.*) Ned. Ned, you understand I never thought it would make all this —— (*Rises, crosses D. to above chair L. of table.*) Is Constance being—her old-maid fussy or is it really unpleasant ——?

CROSSMAN. It is unpleasant. She loves the girl, and she's worried for her.

NICK. (*Groans.*) If I could do something ——

CROSSMAN. (*Crossing L. above NICK to U. R. of sofa.*) You did; but don't make too much of it.

NICK. (*Sincerely. The first kind word he's heard.*) Thank you, boy.

CROSSMAN. (*With contempt.*) Or too little. (NICK *crosses R., sits R. of table.*) Nobody will blame you too much. (*Crosses R. to above chair L. of table.*) The girl's a foreigner and they don't understand her and therefore don't like her. You're a home-town boy and *as such* you didn't do anything they wouldn't do. Boys will be boys and in the South there's no age limit on boyishness. You'll come off all right. But then I imagine you always *do*.

NICK. You think this is coming off all right?

CROSSMAN. No, I don't.

77

NICK. (*Sincerely.* CROSSMAN *stops.*) I didn't even want her. Never thought of her that way.

CROSSMAN. (*Crossing* R. *to above table. Too sympathetic.*) That is too bad. Better luck next time. You're young—in spirit. (*Crosses* U. *He exits into hall toward dining-room as* HILDA, *carrying jewel case and hat box, comes down steps. She has on her hat and gloves.*)

NICK. (*Who is sitting on a line with door and sees her, rises and speaks in German.*) [Where are you going?] *Wobin geben Sie?* (*Crosses* U. *a step.*)

HILDA. (*Crossing* D. *to* C. *of hall door. In German.*) [Good morning, sir. I am taking madam's luggage to the nine-thirty train.] *Guten Morgen, Mein Herr. Ich trage das Gepaeck der gnaedigen Frau zum neun-ubr-dreissig Zug.* (*She moves off* R. NICK *crosses* D. R., *sits, as* NINA *appears.* NINA *has on a hat and gloves. On her heels is* ROSE *in a fluffy negligee.* ROSE *is talking as she follows* NINA *down steps.*)

ROSE. I'm not trying to excuse him. (*Stops on 1st step.*) Nina, you know what young girls are with a tipsy man. I saw them this morning and he didn't have the slightest interest in her. Nina ——

NINA. (*Puts on gloves. Turns to her at foot of stairs. Coolly.*) I know it's eccentric of me, Mrs. Griggs, but I dislike being called by my first name before midnight.

ROSE. (*Hurt, softly.*) You shouldn't allow yourself such a nasty snub. I know Nick well enough to know that he didn't do a thing —— (NINA *laughs.*) He's been my good friend. I'm trying to be a friend to him.

NINA. You will have every opportunity.

NICK. (*Very angry.*) Will you please not stand there in the hall discussing me?

ROSE. Oh! (*Looks at* NICK, *then at* NINA, *turns on step, calls toward kitchen.*) Leon! Could I have my tray upstairs? (*As she goes upstairs.*) Anybody seen my husband this morning? (*Exits upstairs.* NINA *starts* R.)

NICK. (*Rises. With quiet dignity.*) Nina. (*Crosses* U. *to* R. *of hall door. She comes in toward above sofa.*) I just want to say before you go that they're making an awful row about nothing ——

NINA. (*Crossing* L. *to above sofa. Wanting to be left alone.*) You don't owe me an explanation, Nick.

NICK. (*Crossing* L. *to* U. R. *of sofa.*) Nothing happened, Nina, I swear. Nothing happened.

NINA. Try out phrases like "nothing happened" on women like Mrs. Griggs.

NICK. (*Smiles.*) I'm sorry as all hell but they sure are cutting up ——

NINA. Well, it is a tasty little story. Particularly for a girl who is going to be married.

NICK. My God, I'd forgotten about the boy. I must say he's an easy boy to forget about. Now I'll have to take *him* out and explain ——

NINA. (*Turns away.*) Don't do that, Nick. He isn't a fool.

NICK. (*Looks around, thinking of anything to keep her in room.*) Shall I get you some coffee, darling?

NINA. (*Crossing* L. *to* L. *of sofa.*) No. Darling will have it on the train. (*She turns.*)

NICK. (*Pleading.*) Nina, I swear I didn't sleep with her.

NINA. (*Glances at him.*) I believe you. The girl doesn't like you.

NICK. (*Crossing* L. *to above* C. *of sofa.*) Doesn't she? She's been very kind to me. She could have raised hell. That doesn't sound as if she doesn't like me. (NINA *laughs. Slightly annoyed.*) Don't laugh at me this morning. (*After a second.*) What can I do for her, Nina?

NINA. You used to send wicker hampers of white roses. With a card saying "White for purity and sad parting."

NICK. Stop being nasty to me. (*Then he smiles, comes toward her to* L. *end of sofa.*) Or maybe it's a good sign.

NINA. (*Crossing* R. *below coffee table to* C. *Sharp, bitterly.*) It isn't. I just say these things by rote. (*Turns at* L. *of chair* L. *of table.*) I don't know how long I'll be in New York, but you can call Horace and he'll take care of the legal stuff for us. (*Starts* U.)

NICK. (*Crossing* R. *above sofa to her as she stops. Contrite.*) I told you last night that I would agree to the separation because I knew with what justice you wanted to leave me.

NINA. (*Coldly.*) That's not at all what you said.

NICK. (*Indignant.*) I was tight. It was what I meant to say ——

NINA. (*Very angry.*) You're lying! You said just what you meant to say: I was to *leave.* And not make you *sick* with my usual begging to come back ——

NICK. Stop, Nina. Take any kind of revenge you want, but——.

please—some other day. (NINA *moves away* R. *slowly, then crosses around below table.*) Don't leave me. Don't ever leave me. We've had good times, wild times. They made up for what was bad and they always will. Most people don't get that much. We've only had one trouble; you hate yourself for loving me. Because you have contempt for me.

NINA. (*At below chair* R. *of table.*) For myself. I have no right ——

NICK. (*Crossing* D. *to* D. R. *of sofa.*) No, nobody has. No right at all.

NINA. (*Crossing* L. *to below chair* L. *of table. Desperately.*) I wouldn't have married you, Nick, if I had known ——

NICK. (*Crossing* R. *to her. Not sentimental but truthful and sweet.*) You would have married me. Or somebody like me. You've *needed* to look down on me, darling. And to be ashamed of yourself for doing it.

NINA. (*Turns slightly* R. *Softly.*) Am I *that* sick?

NICK. I don't know about such *words*. You found the man you deserved. That's all. I am no better and no worse than what you really wanted. You *like* to—to demean yourself. And so you chose me. You must say I haven't minded much. Because I've always loved you and *knew* we'd last it out. Come back to me, Nina, without shame in wanting to. (*Gently takes her by both arms.*) Put up with me a little longer, kid. I'm getting older and I'll soon wear down. (*He leans down, kisses her neck.*)

NINA. (*She smiles, touched.*) I've never heard you speak of getting old.

NICK. (*Quickly changing subject. Enthusiastically.*) The *Ile* sails next week. Let's get on. We'll have fun. Tell me we're together again and you're happy. Say it, Nina, quick.

NINA. (*Almost a sigh.*) I'm happy. (*He takes her in his arms, kisses her.*)

NICK. (*Crossing* L. *to below coffee table.*) If we could only do something for the kid. Take her with us, get her out of here until they get tired of the gossip ——

NINA. (*Laughs.*) I don't think we will take her with us.

NICK. Ah, now. You know what I mean.

NINA. (*Crossing* L. *to him. Playfully.*) I know what you mean—and we're not taking her with us.

**NICK.** I suppose there isn't anything to do. (*Crosses around chair above to* U. R. *sofa.*) I feel sick, Nina.

**NINA.** (*Crossing* L. *to behind chair* L. *of sofa.*) You've got a hangover.

**NICK.** (*Holds back of neck and punches back with other hand.*) It's more than that. I've got a sore throat and my back aches. Come on, darling, let's get on the train.

**NINA.** You go. I'll stay and see if there's anything I can do. That's what you really want. Go on, Nicky. Maybe it's best. (*Crosses to above* U. L. *of sofa.*)

**NICK.** (*At* U. R. *of sofa.* ) I couldn't do that.

**NINA.** (*Crossing* R. *to* C. *of sofa.*) Don't waste time, darling. You'll miss the train. I'll bring your clothes with me. (*He looks at her, shakes head.*)

**NICK.** (*Laughs, ruefully.*) If you didn't see through me so fast, you wouldn't dislike yourself so much. (*Comes to her. Sincerely.*) You're a wonderful girl. It's wonderful of you to take all this on ——

**NINA.** (*Backs away a step. Ruefully.*) I've had practise.

**NICK.** (*Hurt.*) That's not true. You know this never happened before.

**NINA.** (*Not blaming, but hoping he'll understand. Smiles.*) Nicky, it always confuses you that the fifth time something happens it varies slightly from the second and fourth. (*Takes his arms, puts head on his chest.*) No, it never happened in this house before. Julie had a husband and Madame Sylvia wanted one. And this time you didn't break your arm on a boat deck ——

**NICK.** This is your day, Nina. But pass up the chance to play it too hard, will you? Take me or leave me now, but don't ——

**NINA.** You're right. Please go, darling. Your staying won't do any good. Neither will mine, but maybe ——

**NICK.** When will you come? I tell you what: you take the car and drive to Mobile. I'll wait for you there at the Battle House. Then we can drive the rest of the way together. Must be somewhere in Mobile I can waste time for a few hours ——

**NINA.** (*Gaily.*) I'm sure. But let's have a week's rest. Now go on.

**NICK.** (*Takes her by her arms. Heartily.*) I love you, Nina. And we'll have the best time of our lives. Good luck, darling. And thank you. (*He kisses her.*) They won't rag you, nobody ever does. We'll get the bridal suite on the *Ile* and have all our meals

81

**in bed.** (*He moves away. With enthusiasm.*) If you possibly can, bring the new portrait with you. I can finish it *now.* And try to get me the old portrait, darling. Maybe Constance will sell it to you . . . (NINA *laughs. He looks at her for a moment, crosses to her.*) All right, all right. You think what you want, but I am what I am. (*Takes her by both arms.*) I love you and you love me and that's that and always will be. (*He kisses her, then exits. She stands quietly.*)

NINA. (*Turns face slightly front.*) And that's that and always will be. (*After a second,* CONSTANCE *appears in hall door.* NINA *stares at her.*) I am very sorry, Constance.

CONSTANCE. (*At* R. *of hall door.*) I am sorry, too, my dear.

NINA. (*At* U. L. *of sofa.*) I don't know what else to say. I wish ——

CONSTANCE. (*Crossing* R., *opens doors, picks up* ROSE'S *bag.*) There's nothing for us to say. Well. Would you like your breakfast on the porch? I'll get it for you. (FREDERICK *comes down steps, carrying valise. Puts it by* U. R. *hall door.*) Shall I send breakfast up to Nick? (*Crosses to* L. *of hall door.*)

NINA. (*Very quickly.*) No, no. I'll just have mine and ——

FREDERICK. (*Crossing to* R. *end of hall door. Calling to* CONSTANCE.) Where's Sophie?

CONSTANCE. (*At* U. C.) I'll send her in.

FREDERICK. (*Smiles.*) Don't sound so solemn, Miss Constance.

CONSTANCE. I didn't mean to. (*She disappears in direction of dining-room, upstage* L. *of stairs.* CARRIE *comes in, from stairs, stands in hall door.*)

NINA. Mr. Ellis, I should be carrying a sign that says my husband is deeply sorry and so am I. (*He smiles at her. She turns, goes out on porch and off upstage.*)

CARRIE. (*Crossing* L. *to below phone table. Hesitantly.*) She's a nice woman, I think. Must be a hard life for her.

FREDERICK. (*Laughs.*) I don't think so. (*Turns as he hears* SOPHIE *in hall. Back* R. *few steps.*) Now remember, Mother. (SOPHIE *appears in door.* FREDERICK *crosses* U. *to* R. *of door, goes to her, takes her arms. Very directly.*) I want to tell you something fast. I don't know how to explain it, but I'm kind of glad this foolishness happened. It makes you seem closer to me, some silly way. I can't make it clear. You must believe that. Now there are two things to do right away. Your choice.

SOPHIE. (*Touches his arm.*) I have made bad gossip for you, Frederick.

FREDERICK. It's a comic story and that's all.

SOPHIE. (*Crossing L. few steps.*) But nobody here thinks it's comic and they will not think so in New Orleans, either. Is that not so, Mrs. Ellis?

CARRIE. (*Crossing a step toward* SOPHIE.) I think you should travel up with us, Sophie. Right now. Whatever is to be faced, we will do much better if we face it all together and do it quickly.

FREDERICK. (*Looks at her, as if they had had previous talk.*) You're putting it much too importantly. There's nothing to be faced.

CARRIE. I didn't mean to make it too important. Of course, it isn't ——

SOPHIE. (*Crossing D. to him. Puts her hand on his arm.*) But, it is important to you.

FREDERICK. (*Shyly.*) Look, as far as I'm concerned the whole foolishness makes us seem less like strangers. I'd hoped you'd feel the same way ——

CARRIE. (*With authority. Quickly. Crosses D. to above sofa.*) Run and pack a bag, Sophie. It's a lovely day for driving.—Now, let's not talk about it any more.

SOPHIE. (*Crossing a step toward her.*) No. My leaving here would seem as if I must be ashamed, and you ashamed for me. I must not come with you today. I must stay here. (*Smiles.*)

FREDERICK. All right. That makes sense. Mother and Grandma will drive up and I'll stay here ——

SOPHIE. (*Crossing to him. Very quickly.*) No, no. You must *not* stay here. (*Points to windows, meaning town.*) They knew you had made plans to leave today as usual. And so you must leave. We must act as if nothing had happened, and if we do that, it will all end more quickly. (FREDERICK *turns* R. *slightly. She turns him back.*) Believe me, Frederick. You know what I say is true. (*To* CARRIE.) You tell him that, please, Mrs. Ellis. (FREDERICK *crosses* R. *to doors.*)

CARRIE. (*Crossing* R. *to* U. R. *of sofa.*) I don't know. You belong with us now, Sophie. We don't want to leave you.

SOPHIE. (*Smiles, very cheerful.*) You are both very kind. But you *know* what I say is best for us all, and of no importance whether I come one week or the next.

CARRIE. (*Crossing to her, shakes hands. With assurance.*) Goodbye, Sophie. We will be waiting for you. (*She exits U. R. MRS. ELLIS enters from hall, crosses D. to U. R. of sofa. FREDERICK crosses D. R. to above D. R. chair.*)

SOPHIE. (*Crossing D. to his L. Smiles.*) This is best. Please.

FREDERICK. Then let me come back this week end. Can I do that?

SOPHIE. (*She touches his face.*) I think so. You are a nice man, Frederick.

FREDERICK. (*Humbly.*) And you're a nice girl to think so. (*Kisses her.*) See you in a few days. (*Turns to go out, passes MRS. ELLIS.*) I feel happy, Grandma. (*Picks up bags, exits U. R. MRS. ELLIS nods, waits for him to exit. SOPHIE sits down chair R. of table.*)

MRS. ELLIS. (*After a second.*) Sophie.

SOPHIE. (*Smiles as if she knew what was coming.*) Yes.

MRS. ELLIS. Did Carrie ask you to leave with us? (*SOPHIE nods.*) Ah. That's not good. When Carrie gets smart she gets very smart. (*Crosses D. to above table.*) Sophie, Frederick meant what he said to you. (*SOPHIE faces front, listening and thinking.*) But I know them both and I would guess that in a week, or two or three, he will agree to go to Europe with his mother and he will tell you that it is only a postponement. And he will believe what he says. Time and decisions melt and merge for him and ten years from now he will be convinced that you refused to marry him. And he will always be a little sad about what could have been.

SOPHIE. Yes. Of course.

MRS. ELLIS. Carrie never will want him to marry. And she will never know it. Well, she, too, got cheated a long time ago. There is very little I can do—perhaps very little I want to do any more. Don't judge him too harshly, child.

SOPHIE. (*Looking front.*) No, I will not judge. I will write a letter to him.

MRS. ELLIS. (*Not sentimental.*) That's my girl. Don't take from us what you don't have to take, or waste yourself on defeat. Oh, Sophie, feel sorry for Frederick. He is nice and he is nothing. And his father before him, and my other sons. And myself. Another way. (*SOPHIE rises, crosses U. to above R. chair.*) Well. (*SOPHIE takes her hands.*) If there is ever a chance, come and see me. (*She moves out U. R. After a second CONSTANCE comes in*

*from hall with breakfast tray. She looks at* SOPHIE. NINA *enters upstage porch, crosses* D., *sits* L. *of table.*)
CONSTANCE. (*Crossing to above sofa.*) Why don't you go up to my room, dear, and lie down for a while? *She's on the porch.* (SOPHIE *crosses* L. *slowly to above* C. *of sofa.* CONSTANCE *crosses to porch, puts tray on small table down stage, then crosses back to living-room and crosses below sofa, gets cup, crosses* U. C. *Hesitantly.*) Carrie just told me you'll be going up to town in a few weeks to stay with them. I'm glad.
SOPHIE. (*At above* C. *of sofa.*) I will not be going to New Orleans, Aunt Constance, and there will be no marriage between Frederick and me.
CONSTANCE. (*Stares at her.*) But Carrie told me ——
SOPHIE. She believes that she wants me today. But it will not be so tomorrow.
CONSTANCE. (*After a second.*) I wish I could say I was surprised or angry. (*Crosses* L. *to her.*) But I'm not sorry. No marriage without love ——
SOPHIE. (*Pleasantly.*) Yes. Yes.
CONSTANCE. (*Gently. Puts hand on* SOPHIE'S *arm.*) You're not to feel bad or hurt.
SOPHIE. (*Touches her arm.*) I do not.
CONSTANCE. I'm —— I'm glad. Mighty glad. Everything will work out for the best. (*Crosses* L. *to her. Gently.*) You'll see, dear. We'll have a nice time.
SOPHIE. (*Almost as if she were speaking to a child.*) Yes, Aunt Constance. (CONSTANCE *exits into hall.* SOPHIE *goes* L. *to upstage of living-room door. Hesitates. Looks back, then crosses to porch. She takes coffee pot, pours* NINA'S *coffee. Pouring coffee.*) You are a pretty woman, Mrs. Denery, when your face is happy.
NINA. And you think my face is happy *this* morning?
SOPHIE. (*Puts coffee pot on table.*) Oh, yes. You and Mr. Denery have had a nice reconciliation.
NINA. (*Stares at her.*) Er. Yes, I suppose so. (NINA *eats breakfast during following speeches.*)
SOPHIE. I am glad for you. That is as it has been and will always be. (*She sits on chair* U. R. *of porch table.*)
NINA. (*Uncomfortably.*) Sophie, if there was anything I can do —— There's no good my telling you how sorry, how —— What can I do?

85

SOPHIE. You can give me five thousand dollars, Mrs. Denery. (NINA *puts coffee on table.*) American dollars, of course. (*Demurely, her accent from now on grows more pronounced.*) I have been subjected to the most degrading experience from which no girl easily recovers. (*In French.*) [A most degrading experience from which no young girl easily recovers ——] Une expérience la plus dégradante de laquelle aucune jeune fille ne peut se remettre.

NINA. (*Stares at her.*) It sounds exactly the same in French.

SOPHIE. (*Bitter but not heavy.*) Somehow sex and money are simpler in French. Well —— (*Moves chair a little closer to* NINA.) In English, then, I have lost or will lose my most beloved fiancé; I cannot return to school and the comrades with whom my life has been so happy; my aunt is now burdened with me for many years to come. I am utterly, utterly miserable, Mrs. Denery. I am ruined. (NINA *bursts out laughing. Firmly, quietly, rather sly.*) Please do not laugh at me.

NINA. I suppose I should be grateful to you for making a joke of it.

SOPHIE. (*Smiling slightly.*) You make a mistake. I am most serious.

NINA. (*Stops laughing.*) Are you? Sophie, it is an unpleasant and foolish incident and I don't wish to minimize it. But don't you feel you're adding considerable drama to it?

SOPHIE. No, ma'am. I did not say that is the way I thought of it. But that is the way it will be considered in this place, in this life. Little is made into very much here.

NINA. (*Sharply.*) It's just the same in your country.

SOPHIE. No, Mrs. Denery. You mean it is the same in Brussels or Strasburg or Paris, with those whom you would meet. In my class, in my town, it is *not* so. In a poor house if a man falls asleep drunk—he is not alone with an innocent young girl because her family is in the same room, not having any other place to go. It arranges itself differently; you have more rooms and therefore more troubles.

NINA. (*Slightly sarcastic.*) Yes. I understand the lecture. (*Pauses.*) Why do you want five thousand dollars, Sophie?

SOPHIE. I wish to go home.

NINA. (*Rises, crossing around to behind her chair. Gently.*) Then I will be happy to give it to you. Happier than you know to think we can do something.

86

SOPHIE. (*Firmly, with pride.*) Yes. I am sure. But I will not accept is as largesse—to make you happy. We will call it a loan, come by through blackmail. One does not have to be grateful for blackmail money, nor think of oneself as a charity girl.

NINA. (*Shocked, not believing. After a second.*) Blackmail money?

SOPHIE. (*Rises, crossing around* R. *to above her chair.*) Yes, ma'am. You will give me five thousand dollars because if you do not I will say that Mr. Denery seduced me last night. (NINA *starts at her, laughs.*) You are gay this morning, madame.

NINA. (*At* L. *of* SOPHIE'S *chair.*) Sophie, Sophie. What a child you are. It's not necessary to talk this way.

SOPHIE. I wish to prevent you from giving favors to me.

NINA. I intended no favors. And I don't like this kind of talk. Nick did not seduce you and I want no more jokes about it. (*Pleasantly.*) Suppose we try to be friends ——

SOPHIE. I am not joking, Mrs. Denery. And I do not *wish* us to be friends.

NINA. I would like to give you the money. And I will give it to you for that reason and no other.

SOPHIE. It does not matter to me what you would like. You will give it to me for my reason—or I will not take it. (*Angrily,* NINA *goes toward door, goes into room, crosses to* U. R. *of sofa, then turns to* SOPHIE, *who has followed to* U. L. *of sofa.*)

NINA. You are serious? Just for a word, a way of calling something, you would hurt my husband and me?

SOPHIE. For me it is more than a way of calling something.

NINA. (*Crossing* R. *to few steps above table.*) You're a tough little girl.

SOPHIE. (*Crossing* R. *to above* C. *of sofa. Calmly.*) Don't you think people often say other people are tough when they do not know how to cheat them?

NINA. (*Angrily.*) I was not trying to cheat you of anything ——

SOPHIE. (*Crossing* R. *to above* U. R. *of sofa. Very sure of herself.*) Yes, you were. You wish to be the kind lady who most honorably stays to discharge her obligations. And who goes off, as she has gone off many other times, to make the reconciliation with her husband. How could you and Mr. Denery go on living without such incidents as me? I have been able to give you a second, or a twentieth, honeymoon.

87

NINA. (*Crossing* D. *to above table. Angrily.*) Is that speech made before you raise your price?
SOPHIE. (*Smiles.*) No. A blackmail bargain is still a bargain. (CROSSMAN *appears in hall, from* U. L., *starts upstairs.* SOPHIE *sees him.*)
NINA. (*Looking at table top.*) How would —— How shall we make the arrangements?
SOPHIE. (*Calling.*) Mr. Ned. (CROSSMAN *crosses to* U. R. *of* SOPHIE. *Pleasantly to* NINA.) Mr. Ned will know what to do.
NINA. (*Crossing* U. *to* R. *of* CROSSMAN. *After a second to* CROSSMAN, *not knowing how to say it.*) I'd like to get a check cashed. It's rather a large check. Could you vouch for me at the bank?
CROSSMAN. Sure. That's easy enough. The bank's just around the corner. (NINA *starts* U.)
SOPHIE. (NINA *stops at* R. *of hall door.*) Would you like me to come with you, Mrs. Denery?
NINA. (*Coldly.*) You know, I think perhaps it's wisest for you to stay right here. You and I in a bank, cashing a check, this morning, could well be interpreted as a pay-off, or blackmail. (*Smiling at* CROSSMAN, *she goes out to front hall door, opens it, stands there.*)
SOPHIE. (*Crossing* D. *to* U. R. *of sofa.*) I will be going home, Mr. Ned.
CROSSMAN. (*Smiles.*) Good. (*Looks at her, turns to stare at* NINA, *turns back, disapprovingly.*) At least I hope it's good. (NINA *exits.*)
SOPHIE. I think it is more good than it is not good. (*He goes out* U. R. *of hall.* SOPHIE *sits* R. *end of sofa.* GRIGGS *enters from windows* R.)
GRIGGS. Good morning.
CROSSMAN. Good morning.
GRIGGS. Good morning, Sophie.
SOPHIE. Good morning. (ROSE *comes down steps. Her manner is hurried, nervous.*)
ROSE. (*Crossing* D. *to above table.*) Oh, Ben, I've been looking everywhere for you. (*Turns, sees* SOPHIE. *Very nervous.*) Oh. Good morning, Sophie.
SOPHIE. (*Rises, crossing* U. *toward hall.*) We have seen each other earlier this morning, Mrs. Griggs. (*Exit into hall.*)
ROSE. Have you heard about it? He's been a disappointment to

me. (*Crosses* D., *sits chair* L. *of table.*) I've been lying on the bed thinking about it. Nick Denery, I mean.

GRIGGS. (*Sits chair* R. *of table.*) I'm sorry.

ROSE. (*Seriously.*) You know, Ben, I've just about come to the conclusion that I'm often wrong about people, mostly men.

GRIGGS. And what did you and Henry—ah—put together, Rose?

ROSE. (*Rises, to* D. L. *of chair. Avoiding the issue.*) It was so hot in town. Henry's got that wonderful air-conditioning, of course, but it's never like your own air. I think Sunday's the hottest day of the year, anyway.

GRIGGS. (*Rises, to below table.*) What point did you come to about my decision?

ROSE. (*Crossing* L. *two steps. Almost trembling, hating to face it. Looks away.*) Decision? Your decision ——?

GRIGGS. (*Tensely.*) Please stop playing the fool. I'm afraid of you when you start playing that game.

ROSE. *You* afraid of *me?*

GRIGGS. Yes, me afraid of you. This very minute. Be kind, Rose, and tell me what has been decided for me.

ROSE. (*Softly, very nervous.*) It wasn't like that. Before I saw Henry I went to see Dr. Wills. I've always been sorry you didn't like Howard Wills. He's known as the best man in the South, Ben.

GRIGGS. (*Growing angry.*) I don't want to hear about Wills. Come to the point. What did you and Henry decide?

ROSE. (*Grows sober, recognizing the tone.*) I've been uneasy. I've sometimes been in pain, all summer. But I guess I knew because I guess I've known since that army doctor in 1934 —— I didn't want to talk about it —— (*Moves toward him, frightened.*) I have bad heart trouble, Ben.

GRIGGS. (*After a second, as if he were sick.*) Don't play that trick, Rose. It's just too ugly.

ROSE. I am not playing a trick. Wills wrote you a letter about it. (*She reaches in pocket of her robe, hands him folded paper. He takes it from her, crosses* R. *few steps, unfolding it, reads it. She backs away* L. *few steps.* GRIGGS *crosses* U. *to* R. *of table before speaking.*)

GRIGGS. (*Crushing letter in his hand. Tensely.*) How much did Henry pay Wills for this? (ROSE *crosses* U. *to* L. *of table before speaking.*)

ROSE. (*Gently, seriously.*) It wasn't bought. Even Henry couldn't buy it. (*She turns, goes toward hall door, upstage, as if she were a dignified woman.* GRIGGS *crosses around table to above it.*)

GRIGGS. (*Softly.*) Tell me about it. (*She turns upstage* C. *of hall door.*)

ROSE. (*Not sentimental or self-pitying, crosses* D. *slowly to* U. R. *corner of sofa.*) There isn't much to tell. I've known some of it for years, and so have you. I just didn't know it was this bad, or I guess I wouldn't have gone there yesterday. Wills says I must lead a—well, a very different life. I'll have to go to the country somewhere and rest most of the day—not climb steps or go to parties or even see people much. I like people, I —— Well, I just don't understand what I can do, except sit in the sun, and I hate sun —— Oh, I don't know. He said worse than I am saying —— I can't say it —— (*Turns* L.)

GRIGGS. Yes. (*After a second.*) I'm sorry.

ROSE. (*Turns back to him. Sincere, simple.*) I know you are. You've been my good friend. I'm frightened, Ben. I play the fool, but I'm not so big a fool that I don't know I haven't got anybody to help me. I pretend about the boys and what they're like, but I know just as well as you do that they're not very kind men and won't want me and won't come to help me. (*With feeling.*) And of course I know about Henry—I always have. I've got nobody and I'm not young and I'm scared. Awful scared.

GRIGGS. You don't have to be.

ROSE. (*Who is crying, very quietly.*) Wills says that if I take good care I might be, probably will be, in fine shape at the end of the year. Please stay with me this year, just this year. I will swear a solemn oath—believe me, I'm telling the truth now—I will give you a divorce at the end of the year without another word. I'll go and do it without any fuss, any talk. But please help me now. I'm so scared. Help me, please.

GRIGGS. (*Comes to her, presses her arm. Looks front.*) Of course. Of course. Now don't let's speak of it again and we'll do what has to be done. (*She turns, goes out upstairs. He stands where he is. A moment later,* CROSSMAN *comes in, stares at* GRIGGS *as if he knew something was wrong. Then he speaks casually.* GRIGGS *crosses to above chair* R. *of table.*)

CROSSMAN. (*Crossing* L. *to* U. L. *of sofa.*) Seen Sophie?

GRIGGS. (*Takes out cigarette. As if it were an effort, idly.*) In the

90

kitchen, I guess. Tough break for the kid, isn't it? (*Lights cigarette.*)

CROSSMAN. (*Smiles, crossing* D. *to* D. L. *of sofa.*) Perhaps it isn't. I don't know. (*Puts envelope in coat pocket. He watches as* GRIGGS *lights cigarette.* GRIGGS' *hands are shaking and as he puts out match, he stares at them.*)

GRIGGS. (*Smiles.*) My hands are shaking.

CROSSMAN. (*Concerned.*) What's the matter?

GRIGGS. (*Crossing* D. *above table, puts match in ash-tray.*) Worst disease of all. I'm all gone. I've just looked and there's no Benjamin Griggs.

CROSSMAN. (*Crossing* D. *to chair* L. *of sofa. After a second.*) Oh, that. And you've just found that out?

GRIGGS. Just today. Just now.

CROSSMAN. (*Sits chair* L. *of sofa.*) My God, you're young.

GRIGGS. (*Laughs.*) I guess I was. (*Slowly, angrily.*) So at any given moment you're only the sum of your life up to then. There are no big moments you can reach unless you've a pile of smaller moments to stand on. (*Crosses* D. R., *then below table.*) That big hour of decision, the turning point in your life, the some day you've counted on when you'd suddenly wipe out your past mistakes, do the work you'd never done, think the way you'd never thought, have what you'd never had—it just doesn't come suddenly. You've trained yourself for it while you waited—or you've let it all run past you and frittered yourself away. (*Shakes head. Sits* L. *of table.*) I've frittered myself away, Crossman.

CROSSMAN. Most people like us.

GRIGGS. (*Berating himself.*) That's no good to me. Most people like us haven't *done anything* to themselves; they've let it be done to them. I had no right to let it be done to *me*, but I let it be done. What consolation can I find in not having made myself any more useless than an Ellis, a Denery, a Tuckerman?

CROSSMAN. Or a Crossman.

GRIGGS. The difference is you're meant to fritter yourself away.

CROSSMAN. And does that make it better?

GRIGGS. Better? Worse? All I know is it makes it different. Rose is a sick woman. You know I'm not talking only about Rose and me, don't you?

CROSSMAN. I know.

GRIGGS. (*In a low voice as if to himself.*) And I don't like Rose.

91

And I'll live to like her less. (CONSTANCE *appears in hall carrying tray. She is followed by* SOPHIE, *who is carrying a carpet sweeper and a basket filled with cleaning rags, etc.* SOPHIE *puts carpet sweeper in hall* R. *of* R. *chair.* CONSTANCE *comes to door. She speaks wearily.*)

CONSTANCE. (*In hall door. To* GRIGGS. GRIGGS *rises, crosses* R. *to above* D. R. *chair.* CROSSMAN *rises, crosses to* L. *of sofa.*) Sorry about Rose's breakfast. I forgot it. Sophie is going to help Rose to get packed. I don't mean to sound inhospitable, but since you were going tomorrow, anyway —— (*Gently.*) I'm just tired and it would be easier for us. Please forgive me but you're an old friend and you will understand.

GRIGGS. (*Crossing* U. *to* L. *of* CONSTANCE. *Smiles, pats her arm.*) Yes, of course. I'll take the tray to Rose. (*He takes it from her, crosses in back of her, goes up steps.* CONSTANCE *comes in room to* R. *of table, sighs.*)

CROSSMAN. (*Crossing* R. *to* U. C.) Sophie. (SOPHIE *comes to him.*) I was asked to give you this. (*He hands her envelope.*)

SOPHIE. Thank you, Mr. Ned.

CONSTANCE. (*Idly, without much interest.*) Secrets?

CROSSMAN. That's right. Secrets. Old love letters or something. (*Crosses* L. *to* L. *of sofa.* SOPHIE *laughs, goes out* U. L. *of hall.*)

CONSTANCE. (*After a silence.*) I hate this house today.

CROSSMAN. Well, they'll all be gone soon.

CONSTANCE. (*Crossing* L. *to* R. *of sofa.*) You won't go? Please.

CROSSMAN. I'll stay for a few days if you'd like me to.

CONSTANCE. Oh, yes. I need you to stay.

CROSSMAN. Don't worry about what the town thinks. Just act as if nothing had happened and they'll soon stop talking.

CONSTANCE. Oh, I'm not worrying about that. I feel so lost, Ned. I mean, right now, if you asked me, I wouldn't know what I thought or believed, or ever had, or —— Well, what have I built my life on? Do you know what I mean?

CROSSMAN. (*Crossing to below* L. *end of sofa.*) Sure, I know. It's painful. (*Sits sofa.*)

CONSTANCE. Sophie will be going back to Europe. She just told me. She *wants* to go. Did you know that?

CROSSMAN. Is that so?

CONSTANCE. (*Sits sofa.*) She wants me to come with her and live with them, but I told her I'd be no happier in a new life than she was. Nick said you wouldn't be coming here next summer. Did you say anything like that, or was it one of Nick's lies? (*No answer.*) Why, Ned?

CROSSMAN. Hasn't anything to do with you, Con. Just think I'd be better off. You know, it's kind of foolish . . . two weeks a year . . . coming back here and living a life that isn't me any more. It's too respectable for me, Con. I ain't up to it any more.

CONSTANCE. Oh. It's what I look forward to every summer. What will I . . . ? Where is Nick? I haven't seen him. I wish they'd leave . . .

CROSSMAN. They've gone.

CONSTANCE. (*Rises, to* R. *of sofa.*) Without a word to me? Exactly the way he left years ago. I didn't ever tell you that, did I? We had a date for dinner. He didn't come. He just got on the boat. I didn't ever tell anybody before. What a fool! (*Crosses* L. *above sofa.*) All these years of making a shabby man into the kind of hero who would come back some day all happy and shining . . .

CROSSMAN. Oh, don't do that. Don't use words like *shabby*. He never asked you to make him what he wasn't. Or wait twenty years to find him out.

CONSTANCE. No, he didn't. That's true. (*Crosses to portrait.*) Do I look like this?

CROSSMAN. You look nice.

CONSTANCE. Look at it.

CROSSMAN. (*Rises, crossing* L. *to behind chair* L. *of sofa.*) No. I don't want to.

CONSTANCE. Much older than I thought or —— And I don't look very bright. (*Puts portrait on chair by phone.*) Well, I haven't been very bright. I want to say something to you. I can't wait any longer. Would you forgive me? (*Crosses* D. *to above sofa.*)

CROSSMAN. Forgive you? For what?

CONSTANCE. For wasting all these years. For not knowing what I felt about you, or not wanting to. Ned, would you have me now?

CROSSMAN. What did you say?

CONSTANCE. Would you marry me? (*Crosses* R. *to* R. *end sofa, sits.* SOPHIE *rounds the corner, singing her song.*) She's happy. That's good. I think she'll come out all right, always.

CROSSMAN. I live in a room and I go to work and I play a game called getting through the day while you wait for night. The night's for me . . . just me . . . and I can do anything with it I want. There used to be a lot of things to do with it, good things, but now there's a bar and another bar and the same people in each bar. When I've had enough I go back to my room . . . or somebody else's room . . . and that never means much one way or the other. A few years ago I'd have weeks of reading . . . night after night . . . just me. But I don't do that much any more. Just read all night long. You can feel good that way.

CONSTANCE. I never did that. I'm not a reader.

CROSSMAN. (*Crossing to below sofa.*) And a few years ago I'd go on the wagon twice a year. Now I don't do that any more. (*Sits sofa.*) And I don't care. And all these years I told myself that if you'd loved me everything would have been different. I'd have had a good life, been worth something to myself. I wanted to tell myself that. I wanted to believe it. Griggs was right. I not only wasted myself, but I wanted it that way. All my life, I guess, I wanted it that way.

CONSTANCE. (*Leaning toward him.*) And you're not in love with me, Ned?

CROSSMAN. (*Putting his hand on hers.*) No, Con. Not now.

CONSTANCE. Let's have a nice dinner together, just you and me, and go to the movies. Could we do that? (*He pats her hand.*)

CROSSMAN. (*Moves closer to her.*) I've kept myself busy looking into other people's hearts so i wouldn't have to look into my own. If I made you think I was still in love, I'm sorry. (*Kisses her hand.*) Sorry I fooled you and sorry I fooled myself. And I've never liked liars . . . least of all those who lie to themselves.

CONSTANCE. Never mind. Most of us lie to ourselves, darling. Most of us.

CURTAIN

94

# PROPERTY PLOT

## Act I

ON STAGE

D. R.:
Chair
Small table
Table lamp (on table)
Ash-tray (on table)
Matches (on table)

U. R.:
Small chair
Desk
Books (on desk)
Candlesticks (on desk)
Vase (on desk)

L. *of Hall Doorway*:
Phone table and chair
Phone (on table)

U. L.:
Bookcase containing books and bric-a-brac
Round table (in U. L. corner)
Lamp (on table)
Phonograph (on table)
Ornamental tray (on table)

D. L.:
Small chair

L. C.:
Sofa with back running from L. end to C. (has arm on L. end)
2 small cushions (on sofa)
Coffee table
Ash-tray (on coffee table)

R. C.:
Small table
2 chairs (on either side of table)

Cigarette box (on table)

*In Hallway*:
Grandfather clock
2 small chairs
Mirror
Hall table
Table lamp (on table)
Vase of flowers (on table)

*On Porch*, U. L.:
Small stand with fern
Porch furniture to match as follows:
  Rocking chair (below fern)
  Medium-sized wicker table (below rocking chair)
  Small armless porch chair (below table)

*On Porch, Downstage*:
Low porch table
2 small chairs

*Hand Props*:
Rosette (Carrie)
Needlework (Carrie)
Galley proofs and pencil (Fred)
Book (Griggs)
New Orleans Paper (Crossman)
Cigarette (Griggs)
Cigarette (Crossman)

OFF STAGE
*Hand Props*, U. C.:
Butler's tray with 6 filled demitasses, container of sugar (Leon)

95

Hand tray with bottle of brandy,
6 brandy glasses (Sophie)
Vase of flowers (Constance)
Portrait of Constance (Constance)
2 sheets ⎫
2 blankets ⎬ (Sophie)
1 pillow and case ⎭

1 bathrobe ⎫ (Sophie)
1 set pajamas ⎭
Overnight case and jewel case
(Hilda)

## Act II—Scene 1

FURNITURE CHANGE AND ON
STAGE PROPS
Small porch table moved to below
wicker table
Easel set up D. L. on porch
Picture of Constance on easel
Box of paints and pallette on
chair L. of and below easel
Bedclothes folded on chair D. L.
of sofa
Carpet sweeper on stage for
Sophie

OFF STAGE
U. C.:
Cigarette (Carrie)
Overnight case (Rose)
Butler's tray with 6 coffee cups
and saucers, coffee pot, cream,
sugar and spoons (Sophie)
Vase of flowers (Sophie)
Empty tray (Sophie)
Large breakfast tray with 2 full
breakfasts (Leon)
Small dinner bell (Leon)
New Orleans Sunday paper
(Crossman)

## Act II—Scene 2

QUICK CHANGE ON STAGE
Tray with 6 champagne glasses to
table R. C. (one glass is a break-
away for Crossman-Nick scene)
(One glass half filled for
Constance)
One glass half filled to coffee
table for Nick
Deck of cards to Constance
Champagne bucket with half-
filled bottle to phone table
Empty champagne bottle to table

U. L.
Portrait from porch to L. of bookcase
Book to Sophie on porch
Large wicker table to original
marks, small porch table to
original marks

Chairs set for opening of Act
II, Scene 2
Strike butler's tray, breakfast tray
and newspaper

OFF STAGE
D. R.:
1 small laurel branch (Nick)
U. C.:
Picnic basket (Griggs)
Car keys (Crossman)
Glass of milk (Sophie)
Book (Sophie)
Bedclothes (Sophie)
2 sheets
2 blankets
1 pillow and case
Silent butler (Constance)

## Act III

ON STAGE
R. C.:
Cup of coffee on table
Strike:
  Champagne bottles
  Bucket and glasses
  Picnic basket
  Cards etc.

OFF STAGE
D. R.:
Overnight case (Rose)

U. C.:
Envelope of money (Crossman)

Note from Dr. Wills (Rose)
Carpet sweeper (Sophie)
Basket of cleaning rags (Sophie)
Silver tray
Coffee pot (on tray) ⎫
Cream (on tray)      ⎬ (Leon)
Sugar (on tray)      ⎭
2 complete breakfast trays (Constance)
Overnight case ⎱ (Hilda)
Jewel case     ⎰
Suitcase (Fred)

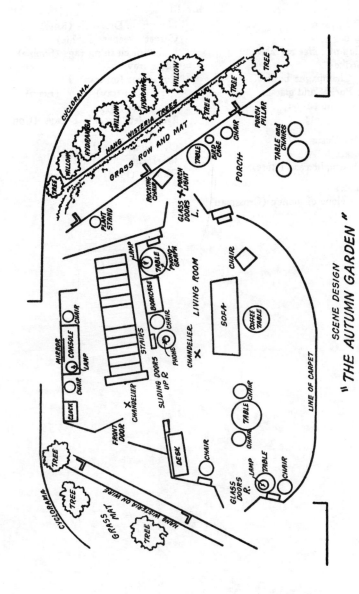

SCENE DESIGN
"THE AUTUMN GARDEN"

# NEW PLAYS

★ **THE CREDEAUX CANVAS by Keith Bunin.** A forged painting leads to tragedy among friends. "There is that moment between adolescence and middle age when being disaffected looks attractive. Witness the enduring appeal of Prince Hamlet, Jake Barnes and James Dean, on the stage, page and screen. Or, more immediately, take a look at the lithe young things in THE CREDEAUX CANVAS..." –*NY Times.* "THE CREDEAUX CANVAS is the third recent play about painters...it turned out to be the best of the lot, better even than most plays about non-painters." –*NY Magazine.* [2M, 2W] ISBN: 0-8222-1838-0

★ **THE DIARY OF ANNE FRANK by Frances Goodrich and Albert Hackett, newly adapted by Wendy Kesselman.** A transcendently powerful new adaptation in which Anne Frank emerges from history a living, lyrical, intensely gifted young girl. "Undeniably moving. It shatters the heart. The evening never lets us forget the inhuman darkness waiting to claim its incandescently human heroine." –*NY Times.* "A sensitive, stirring and thoroughly engaging new adaptation." –*NY Newsday.* "A powerful new version that moves the audience to gasps, then tears." –*A.P.* "One of the year's ten best." –*Time Magazine.* [5M, 5W, 3 extras] ISBN: 0-8222-1718-X

★ **THE BOOK OF LIZ by David Sedaris and Amy Sedaris.** Sister Elizabeth Donderstock makes the cheese balls that support her religious community, but feeling unappreciated among the Squeamish, she decides to try her luck in the outside world. "...[a] delightfully off-key, off-color hymn to clichés we all live by, whether we know it or not." –*NY Times.* "Good-natured, goofy and frequently hilarious..." –*NY Newsday.* "...[THE BOOK OF LIZ] may well be the world's first Amish picaresque...hilarious..." –*Village Voice.* [2M, 2W (doubling, flexible casting to 8M, 7W)] ISBN: 0-8222-1827-5

★ **JAR THE FLOOR by Cheryl L. West.** A quartet of black women spanning four generations makes up this hilarious and heartwarming dramatic comedy. "...a moving and hilarious account of a black family sparring in a Chicago suburb..." –*NY Magazine.* "...heart-to-heart confrontations and surprising revelations...first-rate..." –*NY Daily News.* "...unpretentious good feelings...bubble through West's loving and humorous play..." –*Star-Ledger.* "...one of the wisest plays I've seen in ages...[from] a master playwright." –*USA Today.* [5W] ISBN: 0-8222-1809-7

★ **THIEF RIVER by Lee Blessing.** Love between two men over decades is explored in this incisive portrait of coming to terms with who you are. "Mr. Blessing unspools the plot ingeniously, skipping back and forth in time as the details require...an absorbing evening." –*NY Times.* "...wistful and sweet-spirited..." –*Variety.* [6M] ISBN: 0-8222-1839-9

★ **THE BEGINNING OF AUGUST by Tom Donaghy.** When Jackie's wife abruptly and mysteriously leaves him and their infant daughter, a pungently comic reevaluation of suburban life ensues. "Donaghy holds a cracked mirror up to the contemporary American family, anatomizing its frailties and miscommunications in fractured language that can be both funny and poignant." –*The Philadelphia Inquirer.* "...[A] sharp, eccentric new comedy. Pungently funny...fresh and precise..." –*LA Times.* [3M, 2W] ISBN: 0-8222-1786-4

★ **OUTSTANDING MEN'S MONOLOGUES 2001–2002 and OUTSTANDING WOMEN'S MONOLOGUES 2001–2002 edited by Craig Pospisil.** Drawn exclusively from Dramatists Play Service publications, these collections for actors feature over fifty monologues each and include an enormous range of voices, subject matter and characters. MEN'S ISBN: 0-8222-1821-6   WOMEN'S ISBN: 0-8222-1822-4

**DRAMATISTS PLAY SERVICE, INC.**
440 Park Avenue South, New York, NY 10016  212-683-8960  Fax 212-213-1539
postmaster@dramatists.com  www.dramatists.com

# NEW PLAYS

★ **A LESSON BEFORE DYING by Romulus Linney, based on the novel by Ernest J. Gaines.** An innocent young man is condemned to death in backwoods Louisiana and must learn to die with dignity. "The story's wrenching power lies not in its outrage but in the almost inexplicable grace the characters must muster as their only resistance to being treated like lesser beings." *–The New Yorker.* "Irresistable momentum and a cathartic explosion…a powerful inevitability." *–NY Times.* [5M, 2W] ISBN: 0-8222-1785-6

★ **BOOM TOWN by Jeff Daniels.** A searing drama mixing small-town love, politics and the consequences of betrayal. "…a brutally honest, contemporary foray into classic themes, exploring what moves people to lie, cheat, love and dream. By BOOM TOWN's climactic end there are no secrets, only bare truth." *–Oakland Press.* "…some of the most electrifying writing Daniels has ever done…" *–Ann Arbor News.* [2M, 1W] ISBN: 0-8222-1760-0

★ **INCORRUPTIBLE by Michael Hollinger.** When a motley order of medieval monks learns their patron saint no longer works miracles, a larcenous, one-eyed minstrel shows them an outrageous new way to pay old debts. "A lightning-fast farce, rich in both verbal and physical humor." *–American Theatre.* "Everything fits snugly in this funny, endearing black comedy…an artful blend of the mock-formal and the anachronistically breezy…A piece of remarkably dexterous craftsmanship." *–Philadelphia Inquirer.* "A farcical romp, scintillating and irreverent." *–Philadelphia Weekly.* [5M, 3W] ISBN: 0-8222-1787-2

★ **CELLINI by John Patrick Shanley.** Chronicles the life of the original "Renaissance Man," Benvenuto Cellini, the sixteenth-century Italian sculptor and man-about-town. Adapted from the autobiography of Benvenuto Cellini, translated by J. Addington Symonds. "[Shanley] has created a convincing Cellini, not neglecting his dark side, and a trim, vigorous, fast-moving show." *–BackStage.* "Very entertaining…With brave purpose, the narrative undermines chronology before untangling it…touching and funny…" *–NY Times.* [7M, 2W (doubling)] ISBN: 0-8222-1808-9

★ **PRAYING FOR RAIN by Robert Vaughan.** Examines a burst of fatal violence and its aftermath in a suburban high school. "Thought provoking and compelling." *–Denver Post.* "Vaughan's powerful drama offers hope and possibilities." *–Theatre.com.* "[The play] doesn't put forth compact, tidy answers to the problem of youth violence. What it does offer is a compelling exploration of the forces that influence an individual's choices, and of the proverbial lifelines—be they familial, communal, religious or political—that tragically slacken when society gives in to apathy, fear and self-doubt…" *–Westword.* "…a symphony of anger…" *–Gazette Telegraph.* [4M, 3W] ISBN: 0-8222-1807-0

★ **GOD'S MAN IN TEXAS by David Rambo.** When a young pastor takes over one of the most prestigious Baptist churches from a rip-roaring old preacher-entrepreneur, all hell breaks loose. "…the pick of the litter of all the works at the Humana Festival…" *–Providence Journal.* "…a wealth of both drama and comedy in the struggle for power…" *–LA Times.* "…the first act is so funny…deepens in the second act into a sobering portrait of fear, hope and self-delusion…" *–Columbus Dispatch.* [3M] ISBN: 0-8222-1801-1

★ **JESUS HOPPED THE 'A' TRAIN by Stephen Adly Guirgis.** A probing, intense portrait of lives behind bars at Rikers Island. "…fire-breathing…whenever it appears that JESUS is settling into familiar territory, it slides right beneath expectations into another, fresher direction. It has the courage of its intellectual restlessness…[JESUS HOPPED THE 'A' TRAIN] has been written in flame." *–NY Times.* [4M, 1W] ISBN: 0-8222-1799-6

**DRAMATISTS PLAY SERVICE, INC.**
440 Park Avenue South, New York, NY 10016  212-683-8960  Fax 212-213-1539
postmaster@dramatists.com  www.dramatists.com

# NEW PLAYS

★ **THE CIDER HOUSE RULES, PARTS 1 & 2 by Peter Parnell, adapted from the novel by John Irving.** Spanning eight decades of American life, this adaptation from the Irving novel tells the story of Dr. Wilbur Larch, founder of the St. Cloud's, Maine orphanage and hospital, and of the complex father-son relationship he develops with the young orphan Homer Wells. "...luxurious digressions, confident pacing...an enterprise of scope and vigor..." –*NY Times.* "...The fact that I can't wait to see Part 2 only begins to suggest just how good it is..." –*NY Daily News.* "...engrossing...an odyssey that has only one major shortcoming: It comes to an end." –*Seattle Times.* "...outstanding...captures the humor, the humility...of Irving's 588-page novel..." –*Seattle Post-Intelligencer.* [9M, 10W, doubling, flexible casting] PART 1 ISBN: 0-8222-1725-2 PART 2 ISBN: 0-8222-1726-0

★ **TEN UNKNOWNS by Jon Robin Baitz.** An iconoclastic American painter in his seventies has his life turned upside down by an art dealer and his ex-boyfriend. "...breadth and complexity...a sweet and delicate harmony rises from the four cast members...Mr. Baitz is without peer among his contemporaries in creating dialogue that spontaneously conveys a character's social context and moral limitations..." –*NY Times.* "...darkly funny, brilliantly desperate comedy...TEN UNKNOWNS vibrates with vital voices." –*NY Post.* [3M, 1W] ISBN: 0-8222-1826-7

★ **BOOK OF DAYS by Lanford Wilson.** A small-town actress playing St. Joan struggles to expose a murder. "...[Wilson's] best work since *Fifth of July*...An intriguing, prismatic and thoroughly engrossing depiction of contemporary small-town life with a murder mystery at its core...a splendid evening of theater..." –*Variety.* "...fascinating...a densely populated, unpredictable little world." –*St. Louis Post-Dispatch.* [6M, 5W] ISBN: 0-8222-1767-8

★ **THE SYRINGA TREE by Pamela Gien.** Winner of the 2001 Obie Award. A breathtakingly beautiful tale of growing up white in apartheid South Africa. "Instantly engaging, exotic, complex, deeply shocking...a thoroughly persuasive transport to a time and a place...stun[s] with the power of a gut punch..." –*NY Times.* "Astonishing...affecting ...[with] a dramatic and heartbreaking conclusion...A deceptive sweet simplicity haunts THE SYRINGA TREE..." –*A.P.* [1W (or flexible cast)] ISBN: 0-8222-1792-9

★ **COYOTE ON A FENCE by Bruce Graham.** An emotionally riveting look at capital punishment. "The language is as precise as it is profane, provoking both troubling thought and the occasional cheerful laugh...will change you a little before it lets go of you." –*Cincinnati CityBeat.* "...excellent theater in every way..." –*Philadelphia City Paper.* [3M, 1W] ISBN: 0-8222-1738-4

★ **THE PLAY ABOUT THE BABY by Edward Albee.** Concerns a young couple who have just had a baby and the strange turn of events that transpire when they are visited by an older man and woman. "An invaluable self-portrait of sorts from one of the few genuinely great living American dramatists...rockets into that special corner of theater heaven where words shoot off like fireworks into dazzling patterns and hues." –*NY Times.* "An exhilarating, wicked...emotional terrorism." –*NY Newsday.* [2M, 2W] ISBN: 0-8222-1814-3

★ **FORCE CONTINUUM by Kia Corthron.** Tensions among black and white police officers and the neighborhoods they serve form the backdrop of this discomfiting look at life in the inner city. "The creator of this intense...new play is a singular voice among American playwrights...exceptionally eloquent..." –*NY Times.* "...a rich subject and a wise attitude." –*NY Post.* [6M, 2W, 1 boy] ISBN: 0-8222-1817-8

**DRAMATISTS PLAY SERVICE, INC.**
440 Park Avenue South, New York, NY 10016  212-683-8960  Fax 212-213-1539
postmaster@dramatists.com  www.dramatists.com